Royal Robbins
TO BE BRAVE

My Life
VOLUME ONE

PINK MOMENT PRESS

CALIFORNIA 2009

"Royal is an inspiration for us all. His love for Yosemite, and all natural areas, flows from his life of adventure and challenge. His reverence for the mountains has an incredibly broad reach. Moving quietly but with a profound impact on those around him, Royal's ethic has spread worldwide."

Mike Tollefson

President, The Yosemite Fund
Former Superintendent, Yosemite National Park

~

"Royal Robbins writes about his life with the same unflinching courage that made him a climbing legend. His story is a welcome look at the human being who dwells within the myth."

Malcolm Margolin

Founder and Publisher, Heyday Books

~

"Royal is a man for all seasons. In the spring of his life he was wise beyond his years, adventurous and ever seeking harmony between man and nature. Now, in the autumn of his life he is a seasoned man of wisdom, filled with character, integrity and a light in his eyes that rivals the sun."

Tom Frost

Climber, Climbing Hardware Designer,
Founder of Frostworks

"When I first met Royal in 1952, he struck me as the genetic combination of John Muir's spiritual appreciation of nature and the passion of an Olympic gold medalist. With that, he forever changed the world of rock climbing in both ethics and accomplishment!"

Jerry Gallwas
Climber, Chemist

∼

"Royal's words shine with warmth, humor and liveliness, and although the stories are personal, the themes are universal."

John Mead
President & CEO, Adventure 16

∼

"Many people have turned to the mountains to escape from the competitiveness of normal life. But competition can be found at the highest levels of any human activity, including climbing. In the 1960s, many of us thought about taking the next step. Royal took that next step more often than anyone."

Glen Denny
Climber, Photographer, Filmmaker

Published in the United States by
Pink Moment Press
P.O. Box 1050, Ojai, California 93024
www.pinkmomentpress.com

Library of Congress: 2009908155
ISBN: 978-0-9825000-1-9

Printed in the United States of America
by Pace Lithographers, Inc., City of Industry, California
www.pacelitho.com

Book design by Anthony Sweeney
Illustrations by Stephen Wright

Front cover photo, Yosemite landscape by Glen Denny;
Concept by René Daveluy with Liz Robbins

Back cover photo by Glen Denny

Mixed Sources
Product group from well-managed
forests, controlled sources and
recycled wood or fibre
FSC www.fsc.org Cert no. SCS-COC-001005
© 1996 Forest Stewardship Council

Printed on FSC certified, recycled paper

10 9 8 7 6 5 4 3 2 2012 2011 2010

For my beloved mother, who has taught me so much
and who has stood by me all these years.

✳

CONTENTS

Yosemite Valley from Wawona Overlook   *Photo: Glen Denny*

ACKNOWLEDGMENTS

I want to first of all thank Liz Robbins for her invaluable work in seeing that this book got finished. She has been a severe taskmaster (which is what it takes) and has seen that I did my part (writing) while she was doing her part (putting it together and finding a publisher). Thanks, Honey. I don't know where I would be without you.

I also want to thank Pat Ament, Edwin Drummond, and especially Glen Denny for their editing help. Thanks to them the book has legs on which to stand. Denny, of course, is a photographer and has recently published a wonderful book of photographs entitled *Yosemite in the Sixties*. Glen's perspicacity extends beyond taking pictures. He is a master of the English language (all three of these guys are) and I learned to fear his oft-repeated phrase, "What do you mean by this?"

Many others have helped along the way, including my mother, my sister, Thomas Ackawie, the American Alpine Club, Phil and Marilyn Bailey, Jim Brigham, Robert Cates, Yvon Chouinard, Nick Clinch, Rene Daveluy, Peggy Denny, Bill Derr, Tom Frost, Jerry Gallwas, Paco Galvez, Frank Hoover, Don Lauria, Joe Lemay, Barbara Lilley, John Long, Malcolm Margolin, Fred Martin, John Mead, Bart O'Brien, Steve Roper, Mike and Natalie Sherrick, Royal Slagle, Louise and Don Stanley, Tony Sweeney, Denise Tijerina, Michael Tollefson, Kirk Visola, Gershon Weltman, Al Wilkes, Ken Wilson, Ellen Wilts, and Stephen Wright.

And, finally, thanks to my adventure-loving publishers, Bob and Susie Bennitt of Pink Moment Press. They are true American entrepreneurs – loving risk and change, and always striving for perfection.

By Steve Roper

Who was this climber with the odd name of Royal Robbins? An upper-crust Englishman? That's what I thought when I first saw it in 1957 in a Sierra Club journal. I was a teenaged climber, devouring every bit of lore I could. But within a few years his name became so familiar in the climbing journals – and so appropriate – that I ceased to worry about it, though I still call him "Roy" when it suits me.

Royal Robbins has been, for most of his life, a visionary.

Climbers worldwide would had to have been asleep to ignore the exploits of Robbins in the 1960s, when he was the guiding light in Yosemite Valley climbing. He is quick to admit that he was neither the best crack climber nor the fastest aid specialist of his day. A few others might have been gifted with more natural talent. But Royal's gift was that of the willful visionary who didn't merely see things differently; he also saw different things. For Royal, this meant possibilities of upping the ante.

His Leaning Tower exploit, explored at length in this volume, stands forever as the boldest solo climb of early North American climbing.

His 1957 first ascent of the face of Half Dome is another, earlier example. An attempt on this fearsome wall in 1955 failed. Most climbers would have said, "That's enough, it's too hard." But Royal knew it could be done, and subsequently he proved it by completing the country's most difficult climb.

He was a visionary who cherished adventure over certainty, and so, inviting controversy, shunned fixed ropes. This ethic was best exemplified by the second ascent of the Nose of El Capitan, a seven-day outing, the longest a party had ever spent on an American cliff without the "umbilical cord" of fixed ropes.

Royal is a visionary writer, not afraid to get personal. One of his articles began with these words: "Some people are bothered by thoughts of decay and death. Not me. Rather, I am obsessed." Regarding female climbers, in 1970 Robbins wrote "If there is any male chauvinism in Yosemite climbing circles (and there is), it has been dealt a severe blow by two young ladies of exceptional talent and energy." Robbins goes on to list their exploits.

One passage in this volume strikes me as a perfect summation of Robbins' philosophy. "It was tough, but that was good for me. It made me stronger." Although this sounds a bit like Nietzsche, our author is eminently sane and non-fanatical. Over and over again he stresses his belief that one can't quit when things look dismal. This is the time to step up.

I am especially pleased to see this book finally appear, for Robbins is a thoughtful and exceptional man, one who has lived a life of adventure and rectitude. I think of him usually as a climber and writer, but he has also been a successful businessman, a splendid husband and father, a river runner, a guide, a fabulous skier – and, as you will read, a one-time bandit. He recalls his early years with a fierce honesty, and I urge him to get to work on the remaining volumes.

The best is yet to come. Go for it, Roy. Time flies!

INTRODUCTION

Greetings. This is the first of a planned series of books about my life. Volume I, with the first and last chapters detailing a solo ascent of the overhanging face of Yosemite's Leaning Tower, chronicles my birth in West Virginia and growing up in Los Angeles, and, of course, my introduction to climbing. The second book goes from meeting the Sierra Club in 1950 through the first ascent of the face of Half Dome in 1957. The third volume takes it from there to the mid-1960s when Liz and I went to Switzerland. The next book describes our time in Switzerland, and return to the States in 1967, as well as the rest of the 1960s with significant climbs in Yosemite and elsewhere. Volume V is about the 1970s when we made our first river trip, started our family, oversaw the business, and ran a climbing school. The sixth book is about my kayaking adventures in California and Chile, and the last is a tale of our business, Royal Robbins, Inc., which was an on-going adventure from 1968 to 1999.

I have been very lucky to have lived through a lot of close calls and have learned that the way you look at things can strongly influence the way they turn out. I hope to communicate this important truth so others won't have to experience those close calls to grow personally. Of course the series is mostly about climbing as I have given my life to the vertical endeavor and it has repaid me in full, but there are other areas too, such as hopping freights, kayaking, business, marriage, and raising a family, that speak of high adventure. So, though I talk a lot about climbing, adventure is the true subject of these books. I hope that the reader will get the message that life is an adventure and that character counts.

Royal Robbins

CHAPTER I

Realm of the Overhang

West Face of the Leaning Tower   *Photo: Glen Denny*

Alone in a sea of granite. Granite to the right and granite to the left. Granite above and granite below. That's the way it's been since yesterday morning when I started up this overhanging wall, the West Face of the Leaning Tower. Glancing between my feet, I see the giant rocks of the talus field. If I dropped a piton, it would fall silently for many heartbeats before bouncing off a boulder 30 feet out from the base of the wall. Rain drenches the forests and cliffs, but I stay dry under my stupendous umbrella. That's why I am here. Even in the rain I can climb on dry rock. But there's no friend to talk to, no partner to lean on. This time it's solitary confinement – tethered to this wall.

Of course I'm here because I want to be. But why do I keep doing things like this? Hints of answers flicker on the edges of my mind, but I don't go there. I might not like the reasons. Besides, it doesn't matter why. All I know is that when I go climbing I am drawn by an overwhelming desire. I imagine it glorious to attack a mountain or a rock wall. I forget about the fear, the tedium, and the pain. But up here you don't forget. Up here reality thumps you over the head. I could get hurt, or killed. Am I nuts? Perhaps, but one thing's for sure – I'm committed. This isn't like running laps around a track, where you can quit whenever you've had enough. The rock on either side is without holds or cracks. I can't traverse off. If I rappel, I'll end up hanging in space on the end of the rope, far out from the wall. The only escape is over the top.

I've been at it for two days now and have, in the late afternoon, reached a point 100 feet above Ahwahnee Ledge, an oasis I left hours ago to climb this pitch number five. Just five more pitches to the top.

Anchoring my rope to the highest bolts, I rappel back to Ahwahnee Ledge. It's going to be a great place to pass the night, but there's no hurry in preparing a bivouac. I have time to relax and rest my mind. Yvon Chouinard says somewhere that, to climb at your best, "you have to quiet your mind." He doesn't say how. And I don't know the trick. Instead of being quiet, my thoughts dart randomly to the past, the future, to what I've done and all the things I want to be. That's no quiet mind.

I try to focus on the landscape in front of me. Two miles to the west I can see Wawona Overlook, the classic Yosemite Valley viewpoint. My mind races back 14 years to the time when I first stood there, gazing in wonder at the scene before me. Four of us boys and our adult leader had come from Los Angeles to check out the Valley for a Boy Scout camping trip. Mr. Bailey, our Scoutmaster, pointed out the landmarks: There, at the head of the Valley, rising above the other rocks, stood Half Dome. Closer to us, Bridalveil Fall dropped down a cliff on the right, making a thin line of white. Above the fall the three Cathedral Rocks rose in giant steps. Across the Valley from the Cathedrals, though, was the biggest eye catcher of all: a giant block of white granite.

"That's El Capitan," Mr. Bailey said. "They'll never climb that one." I thought about that remark for a moment and then asked, in all innocence, "Why not?"

"Well, just look at it. There's nothing to hang onto. It's too smooth. People can climb mountains, but not a wall like that. It's obviously impossible."

I had to agree. To my 14-year-old eyes those giant sheer walls were indeed the definition of the impossible. I couldn't have dreamed that one day I would actually climb El Capitan or that I would be where I now am.

Looking out over the trees and meadows from my perch on the Tower, I can make out a dozen cars and several buses in the overlook parking lot. A lot of people have arrived for the classic view they have seen only in photographs. This time they're out of luck. On this rainy day in the middle of May, the view doesn't match the pictures. It's a gray day in the postcard paradise of Yosemite Valley. With the cloud ceiling at 6,000 feet, Half Dome is invisible. El Capitan looms gigantic, its reign indisputable, but its head is in the clouds.

The spectators at the overlook can at least enjoy Bridalveil Fall pouring out of its hanging valley. Swollen by snowmelt and rainwater courtesy of a stormy spring, Bridalveil is gushing forth, fat and frothy, to fall hundreds of feet before exploding onto the final rocks in a blizzard of swirling spray. The overlookers can see the fall, and they can see the Leaning Tower just south of it, but they can't see and don't imagine a lone loony lurking in the lean of the Tower.

Gazing down at the Bridalveil parking lot I can make out vehicles but no people. A few minutes ago tourists were milling about down there, eager to get close to the base of the thundering, 600-foot waterfall. Now, to escape the intermittent rain, they have returned to the shelter of their cars. Between showers, one of those spectators could, with binoculars, easily look up and spot me as a fly on the wall. More a spider than a fly, with a web of ropes and slings securing me to the rock. But no one is looking. Tourists come to see cascading water, not a tiny, inchworm man. If someone told them, "There's a guy up there," they would most likely reply, "You must be kidding" or "Is he crazy?"

Perhaps, but I comfort myself with Chesterton's words: "The adventures may be mad, but the adventurer must be sane." Up here I need to be a hardheaded realist. I think I am. Concentrating on placing pitons and arranging self-belays, I fancy myself, if crazy, at least mountain-crafty. All of my skills are focused on coping with what the glaciers have created.

A FACE OF GRANITE, LISTING TO THE WEST

The story of Yosemite Valley and the Leaning Tower is a tale of moving ice. Glaciers unearthed and shaped all the great Yosemite rocks. Over a million years, as the climate repeatedly warmed and cooled, rivers of ice, spilling again and again from the High Sierra, plowed the Tenaya and Merced canyons to reach Yosemite Valley. Joining forces west of Half Dome, the two unstoppable currents became a single stream of frozen water thousands of feet deep. Carrying away earth and rock, the icy mass, inch by inch, sculpted the Incomparable Valley.

When the glaciers passed between El Capitan and the Cathedral Rocks, they spread to the south, grinding against the cliffs, plucking away weaker layers of rock from the Leaning Tower's West Face. This steady quarrying produced a blade of granite that looms over the Valley like Moby Dick in full breach. Its giant thrust taunts the tiny climber, awakening in his heart the latent Ahab.

Ascending the northeast slope in the 1920s, Charles Michael was the first to climb the Leaning Tower. Although modern equipment now makes light work of his route, Michael's solo ascent was a bold adventure back then. Several other routes were put up in the 1940s and 1950s, but climbers never considered – or quickly dismissed – the fearsome West Face. But in 1960, Warren Harding, famous for his first ascent of El Capitan in 1958, turned his attention to the Tower. The West Face was a natural for Harding – overhanging and blank, just his cup of tea. Once Warren got the Tower in his sights there was no stopping him. He gathered a team and began the attack in December 1960, reaching the top with Glen Denny and Al Macdonald in October 1961, by way of the continuously overhanging wall.

Two days ago, when I began clipping doubtful bolts at the bottom of the West Face, the image of Harding, laughing maniacally and flourishing a bottle of red wine, began to dog my thoughts. He hasn't left me. We began as partners on a new route at Tahquitz Rock in southern California. Climbing together, Warren and I quickly became friends. We just as quickly became rivals after Jerry Gallwas, Mike Sherrick, and I made the first ascent of the Northwest Face of Half Dome in June 1957. It was a route Harding wanted. In 1955 Warren had been on an attempt with Jerry, Don Wilson, and me. He was going to be with us for a try in 1956, but those plans never materialized. The next year he was in Alaska, so we formed a new team without him. But he returned to California with Half Dome still on his mind. When he arrived in the Valley with new partners, we were already on the wall. Had we failed, Warren, Mark Powell, and Bill Feuerer, in the old-fashioned tradition of first-ascent competition, were ready to pounce upon the route. They probably would have made it if we hadn't gotten there first.

For Warren it must have been painful to miss out on that first ascent. He might well have sulked. Instead, he hiked 8 long miles to the top of Half Dome to congratulate us, bringing sandwiches, orange juice, and self-deprecating jokes, displaying no evidence of a grudge. He was all smiles and goodwill, probably because he had already replaced Half Dome with an even bigger dream. Within a couple of weeks, Harding was strung out on a climb that would make everyone forget about Half Dome – the 3,000-foot face of El Capitan. His history-making success on the "Nose" of El Cap, the most elegant line in Yosemite, if not the world, was an achievement that removed any doubt about Harding's abilities and determination. It was a powerful move on the chessboard of Yosemite climbing.

This first ascent of El Cap by Harding, Wayne Merry, and George Whitmore, in November 1958, was celebrated by both the climbing press and the general public. Articles about the triumph appeared in men's sport and adventure magazines. Billboards advertising Busch Bavarian Beer featured Harding's muscular torso shouldering a coiled rope while mountains towered in the background. Harding became a national hero, but I wasn't among the applauding throng. I found fault with Warren for using fixed ropes from bottom to top and taking 17 months to do it. I was also galled that he had milked the year-and-a-half spectacle for every possible drop of publicity. It didn't seem right to use climbing that way. How much of my pique was idealism and how much just envy? I don't know. I didn't need the public's eye, yet I was secretly peeved when Warren got it and I didn't. I suppose that if I were really free from the fame dragon, I would have been unaffected by Harding's publicity mongering and by his success on El Capitan. So let's call it mostly envy. Now, as I hang here alone on the Leaning Tower, four and a half years later, I find myself speaking to Warren in my mind, as though he were here with me.

You love that attention, Harding. You love to be in the spotlight. You want it all – to be the best climber and to have the public love you as well. OK, El Cap is yours. I might have hiked to the top to congratulate you, as you did us, but I was in the army. And if I had been in Yosemite? I don't know. I might have sat that one out, seething in the Valley.

Your climb was epic. And strung out the way it was, it made good fodder for the newspapers. You went through a lot of partners. They all dropped out for one reason or another – the relentless exposure, the endless labor hauling loads, climbing miles of fixed lines, worrying about rats gnawing on the ropes.

I admire your grit, Warren. You kept hammering away for a year and a half, and finished the job by bolting all night up the summit overhang.

You climbed El Capitan as they climb Everest, placing camps higher and higher, connecting them with ropes attached to pitons and bolts, until you were close enough to make a summit dash. Some of us don't like that way of getting up Yosemite walls. But I have to admit we weren't ready to believe, back then, that the Big Daddy could be done without fixed ropes.

That instant fame made you hungry for more walls, the smoother the better. You used the El Cap technique on the East Face of Washington Column, reaching the top with Chuck Pratt and Glen Denny.

Then you did the West Face of the Leaning Tower with Denny and Al Macdonald. Al wrote it up in a fine article in the Sierra Club Bulletin. I had no quarrel with his essay, but I did with editor Dave Brower. In the same issue of the Bulletin, our climb of the Salathé Wall got only one page. I wrote a letter to Brower questioning his judgment. Thank heaven that letter never got published.

So, that's how it's been, right? We did Half Dome. You topped it with the Nose. We answered with the Salathé, and you knocked off the Tower. I complained about your fixed ropes, and you just put up more of them. It reached the point where I began to imagine you a prancing figure in a black cape with horns and a pointed tail, jeering and chanting "Semper farcissimus! Semper farcissimus!" Maybe you're right. We mustn't take this stuff too seriously. Looking back, it's more like comedy than tragedy. Sometimes I think we're both mad as hatters.

I don't like your methods, but I love your attitude. You don't care what anyone thinks. And you don't give up. You're a persistent devil! You stick to a wall like pasta al dente.

Interrupting my silent monologue, I gaze upward, craning my neck to scan the final 500 feet of smooth, overhanging wall, studded with roofs. It's a long way to the top. Once again I ask myself, why did I come alone? I could have found a partner. I could have brought enough ropes to leave escape lines. But no, I have to stick my neck out. I have to "see what I am made of." Not very smart if I end up getting killed or having to be rescued.

Warren, you get to the top any way you please. I say you get more points when you're as close to naked as possible. I admit my stunt on the

Tower is meant to be a blow for our side. You used fixed ropes, took your time, and had a team. I'm alone, I can't rappel, and I've got to get up in a few days before my strength gives out. You got here first; I can't take that away, but I can steal some of your bragging rights by raising the style ante. It's another move on the Yosemite chessboard.

We'd probably be buddies except for this thing about climbing. I don't attack you personally, only the way you do it. For me it's all philosophy. For you it's a big joke, like when you skewer me as a kind of preacher, a "Valley Christian."

You're proud of your reputation for boozing and for bedding women. You like to be thought of as one of Old Scratch's true sons. If others are going to wear the white hat, you'll sport the black. How you relish the role of fallen angel!

HARDING MEETS THE LEANING TOWER

Harding's compulsion to climb the West Face of the Leaning Tower sprang from its brute implacability. The wall had no weaknesses. That very invulnerability, daunting to most climbers, exerted a magnetic pull on the steel of Harding's resolve. He'd be damned if he would let himself be intimidated. A giant, featureless wall was, to Warren, a sort of personal affront. It bothered him. It captured his mind. The only way to exorcise the demon was to climb the thing. Harding attacked.

Overshadowed by the gigantic yet graceful Middle Cathedral Rock, and dwarfed by the soaring expanse of El Capitan's calm majesty, the Leaning Tower fails to arrest the imagination the way it

Harding on the Tower   *Photo: Glen Denny*

would if its dominant neighbors didn't loom nearby. Nevertheless, the Tower is a giant eyetooth fanging the sky at the entrance to Yosemite Valley. As Warren found out early in his effort to climb the Tower, this tooth can bite.

Harding was leading near the top of the first pitch. Al Macdonald describes the incident in lively prose:

After pounding in a small expansion bolt, he gained three more feet. Just above his head was another loose flake. In delicate balance, he carefully tested it. Deciding against pitons, he prepared to place another bolt, when without warning the flake broke off and crashed down on his head.

"Dammit! Dammit!" Warren's angry and painful words broke the silence.

"Warren! What happened? Are you hurt?"

A moan was the only reply.

I tied off the belay line and got out prusik slings. If he was unable to help himself we had only a short time to reach him before he would strangle in his own safety rope.

"Warren!" Les [Wilson] yelled again.

"My neck. I think it's broken."

"Do you want me to come up and lower you down?" I called.

"I don't know. Let me rest a second."

Small flecks of blood floated down. "You'd better go up, Al," Les said.

What a stinking mess, I thought. With adrenaline and butterflies both working on me at once, I tied the prusik loops to the climbing rope.

"I think I can make it down okay," said Warren.

"Be sure," I said. "How's your neck? Can you move your head at all?"

"Yeah. All the way around. I can see pretty good too – two of everything."

What a relief! That sounded like the old Warren. The situation which could very easily have had disastrous results was under control. After a careful and cautious retreat, we rushed Warren to the hospital where six or seven stitches were required to close the wound in his head. This incident put a rather ominous end to our first attempt.

After the accident, winter storms protected the Tower from Harding's forays. Six months passed before he and Macdonald returned. The second attempt began in June 1961. Harding led the way, drilling holes for bolts, placing pitons where he could. Every vertical foot was gained by direct-aid climbing. On the second day, after eight strenuous hours, Harding was rewarded with only 35 feet of vertical progress. At the end of each day, they descended fixed ropes and slept in the Valley.

George Whitmore and Glen Denny soon joined the party. Whitmore had been a member of the El Cap summit team. Denny, a tall contrast to the diminutive Harding, was particularly adept at direct-aid climbing. With Glen available, Warren could switch leads and avoid the strain of being 100 percent on the sharp end of the rope. On the fifth day, Harding and Denny reached a ledge at last, and what a ledge it was – horizontal and with room to sleep the entire team. They named it Ahwahnee Ledge after Yosemite's luxury hotel. Macdonald called it "a monumental piece of luck and a real dent in the Tower's armor."

On the other hand, above Ahwahnee Ledge, "the Tower's defenses multiplied." A series of roofs between them and the summit sapped their will to climb. The unbearable June heat clinched the matter, and they bid adios for the summer.

Returning in early October, they found their fixed ropes swaying in the breeze. Whitmore was not available, but Al, Glen, and Warren pushed ahead into the realm of the overhang. Warren and Glen swung leads throughout the upper section. Using Ahwahnee Ledge as an advanced base camp, they worked higher and higher. On October 13, Harding led the last pitch, overhanging to the end. They were up. The siege was ended. The West Face of the Leaning Tower, the steepest big wall ever climbed, was theirs.

The Leaning Tower

Photo: Ed Cooper

CHOOSING THE TOWER, MAY 8, 1963

It's been raining or snowing every day for weeks. Who's ever seen a Yosemite spring like this? When is it going to stop? For us climbers, pinned to the Valley floor, it's frustrating. Many have left to seek the southern California sun at Tahquitz or Joshua Tree. A few climbers are still here, hoping the rain will finally stop, thinking it has to.

Liz and I also hang on. Since the beginning of April, between storms, I've been climbing the walls. I am fit and ready to climb again, but the storms don't seem to have a "between" any more. We pass the days drinking coffee and reading in the Yosemite Lodge cafeteria. The caffeine is adding a buzz to my natural restlessness and beginning to give me crazy ideas, like going up in the rain. Well, why not? A bit of mucking about in the wet will make climbing on dry rock seem easy. At least I'll be doing something.

But which route? The walls are running with water, so free climbing is out of the question. It has to be direct aid, using pitons and slings. Some possible targets are Rixon's Pinnacle, El Cap Tree, Lost Arrow Spire, the Leaning Tower... the Leaning Tower? Now there's a thought. Why climb in the rain when you can stay dry on the Tower's overhanging face? Or nearly dry. The West Face of the Leaning Tower! It's been climbed only once. What a solo! Can I do it?

Curious as to what Liz might think, I run the notion past my levelheaded fiancée. She gives me a surprised look, and then gazes out the Lodge window at the rain. "Hmmm.... You know, you just might.... Yes, of course you can. That would really be something! Besides," she adds, eyes sparkling and smile flashing, "you'll be more fun when you get it out of your system."

She knows I'll get cranky if I don't touch rock soon. But her trust erases any lingering uncertainties. If this woman believes in me, how can I doubt myself?

The next morning we drive 3 miles to the Bridalveil Fall parking lot and peer upward through the rain. It only takes a glance to confirm that, through all the storms, the West Face has stayed dry. Now there are no excuses. I'll go up. With that decision made, I find myself looking ahead to four or five days of short rations: "What say we treat ourselves to breakfast at the Ahwahnee?" "Why not?" Liz answers. She knows the famous hotel intimately, having worked there as dining room hostess in 1960, when we first met.

We leave the Bridalveil parking lot and drive east, first beneath the Cathedral Rocks, and then under the towering North Wall of Sentinel Rock. When we come to the broad expanse of Sentinel Meadow, Liz pulls the car to the side of the road. High on a cliff across the Valley, the awesome torrent of Upper Yosemite Fall pours through a deep notch. We roll down the windows. Although the fall is a mile away, we can easily hear the pounding thunder of the tremendous cataract. Dazzled, we follow the road bridging the Merced River, drive past the market, and then turn east toward the Church Bowl cliffs. A wooden sign announces the gateway to the well-kept grounds of the Ahwahnee Hotel.

The road becomes a narrow lane under a thick canopy of incense cedars, oaks, and pines leading to the Ahwahnee parking lot. Getting out of the car, we glance up to see the Royal Arches streaming with cascades and waterfalls. It's a feast for the eyes, but I shudder to think of that frigid water running down my back. Not to worry. I'll stay dry in the Tower's rain shadow.

We turn toward the hotel. A red carpet leads down the outside passageway to the stately foyer. From there we amble to the Ahwahnee's awesome dining room, where a 35-foot-high ceiling is supported by giant timbers strapped together with bands of wrought iron. These trusses rest on pillars formed of granite blocks. The room has the air of a great cathedral, except the walls are decorated not with Christian icons but with American Indian motifs and designs. The dining hall, like the Ahwahnee itself, is on a scale that dwarfs human visitors. It isn't size alone, however, that impresses, but, as with the surrounding Valley, size combined with grace and proportion.

It's a treat merely to be in the dining room, but what a place for breakfast! Our hostess seats us on the south side next to a 15-foot-high window. It is made of a single sheet of glass. How did they get it here in one piece back in 1927? The waitress, our friend Reva, arrives quickly to take our orders and pour coffee. We silently sip the steaming black brew, gazing through the window at meadows and trees and up at the cliffs below Glacier Point.

When Reva arrives with breakfast we turn our attention from the landscape to bacon and eggs. As we eat, I silently ponder what it will mean to be alone on the Tower.

"What are you thinking?" Liz suddenly asks, breaking into my mood of brooding reflection. I love her for that. I love her for not letting me alone, for insisting I come out and play in the world of real people. In certain moods, I have to be dragged from the comfort zone of my own thoughts.

Surprised by the unexpected question, I mumble, "Oh, ah... I was just running through all the things that might go wrong, just to be sure I have the answers. I know I can do the climbing, but I have never taken a fall while soloing, so I was working that out. Again."

"So, how *are* you going to belay yourself?"

I explain the workings of a rather elaborate system I had developed on a couple of short aid climbs. "I'll slide a couple of prusiks along the belay rope as I move up. They'll be attached to my swami belt. If I fall, the knots should grab the rope and stop me. Then I should be able to climb back up the rope and try again."

"I heard two 'shoulds.' That's two too many."

"You know how careful I am."

"Of course I do. Otherwise I wouldn't let you go. But I'll keep an eye out. If you get in trouble I'll call the rangers."

"No, not the Park Service. We don't want the rangers involved if we can help it. Besides, what could they do?"

I wonder what even my talented climbing brethren could do if I have an accident, but I keep that thought to myself. The main thing is to not need rescuing.

"Boy, these eggs are delicious," I observe, steering talk away from climbing while mopping my plate with a slice of whole-wheat toast. Reva refills our cups with hot, black coffee.

We've got to keep this secret. If word gets out that a lone climber is attempting the overhanging face of the Leaning Tower, crowds will arrive to gape and wonder. This contest is between the Tower and me, and I don't want the distraction of a parking lot full of rubberneckers.

"The story is that I've gone to Berkeley to get more climbing equipment."

"Don't worry, I know how to handle it."

Of course she does.

Reva brings the bill – not too punishing considering the service, the setting, and the quality of the food. We leave the modest sum and then walk with a light step from the great hall. Well rested and well fed, I am ready to grapple with the looming presence 5 miles to the west. Liz knows she has already played a key part in the climb. Without her inspiration I would remain chained to the Valley floor.

We find Camp 4 nearly deserted. At the west end, someone is poking at a smoky campfire. To the east a car is parked next to a tent. Otherwise, we have the place to ourselves. The rain has stopped, but the ponderosa pines continue dripping. It's a dark and cheerless campground but we don't mind the gloom: we have work to do. Liz drives off to shop for food, while I begin sorting climbing gear.

Choosing equipment for a climb like this requires finely balanced decision-making, weighing the competing claims of minimal weight against the importance of having precisely the right tool at the right time – a skyhook, a rurp, even a spare prusik loop. I select two ropes, each 150 feet in length – a light 9 mm and a full-weight 11 mm. I also pick out 50 pitons, 40 carabiners, various slings, warm clothing, and a waterproof pullover. Knowing Harding's team removed some of the lower bolts for use higher up, I add a small bag of spare bolts and hangers. I also take a drill in case any hole or fixed bolt on the wall is unusable.

Liz returns from the Yosemite Market with the bivouac food: salami, bread rolls, nuts, gumdrops, M&M's, and raisins. We mix the nuts, raisins, M&M's, and gumdrops together in a nylon stuff sack. This blend, for some reason called gorp, plays a major role in big-wall meals. Liz has also thoughtfully bought a half pound of Monterey

Jack cheese, a welcome luxury thanks to the cool weather. Normally the cheese would melt in the Valley heat. I now realize that these conditions, which have grounded or driven away all the climbers in Yosemite, are perfect for the one climb I have chosen. I toss in a can of tuna in case I'm up there longer than anticipated.

With the temperatures in the 30s and 40s, I will take only one quart of water per day instead of the usual quart and a half. I optimistically pack five quarts. That should be enough. I can't imagine being up there for six or more days. I cram the food, water, and bivouac gear into a tough canvas pack. I don't bother to pad it against abrasion; it's going to be hanging free most of the time. By evening all is prepared.

As night arrives, the remaining few Camp 4 residents wander over to the Lodge cafeteria or the lounge, leaving us alone under the still-dripping pines. It's chilly, but the tarp over our table keeps us dry.

Liz announces a surprise: "I got us a treat." "What's that?" I ask. She answers by unwrapping a white package revealing two T-bone steaks! These she fries on our Coleman stove, removing hers when it is medium rare and allowing mine to darken to my desired taste – "medium well" in my words, "cooked to a crisp" in hers. The beef really satisfies, especially when washed down with a bottle of red wine. Then to bed, but not to sleep.

Throughout the night I toss and turn, attempting to answer questions that keep me awake with their incessant drumming: Did I forget anything? Do I have enough bolt hangers? What if I drop the pack? What if I break my hammer? Breaking a hammer would be like breaking an arm. I'd have to be rescued. I'll take a spare hammer. Hour after hour I vainly seek sleep. Just as I finally grasp it and am settling into oblivion, the alarm jolts me awake.

These early morning starts are tough. Instead of getting up, I stay in my sleeping bag, thinking. The lure of the sack is overcoming the pull of the peak. I want to snuggle up with Liz. I was braver last night, after that steak and several glasses of wine. Now I'm not so sure. Didn't Napoleon say something about how hard it was to be brave in the early morning? What was it – "2 a.m. courage"? Something like that.

Hovering on the edge of sleep, I try to dream up good reasons for not going. After 15 minutes I give up – I can't think of any honorable ones. I'm not sick, and I've made a commitment, so I drag myself from the tent.

Liz cheerfully rises, brews a pot of coffee, pulls out two packages of Danish pastries, and knifes through the cellophane wrappers. It's a simple breakfast, unlike yesterday morning's feast. She then drives us through a gray dawn to the Bridalveil Fall parking lot.

There it is, looming above: the Leaning Tower, its summit shrouded in mists. I kiss Liz goodbye, put on my pack, and shoulder the two coiled ropes. As I step from the asphalt onto the forest floor, all is still. No leaf stirs; there's no hint of a breeze. Menace hangs in the air, as before a lightning bolt or cloudburst. Neither occurs, so I trudge on.

I come to the edge of the talus and begin scrambling through the jumble of rocks. Moving mechanically, thoughts on the wall above, I carelessly step on a patch of wet lichen atop one of the boulders. My foot skids out and I come down hard on my right side before bouncing off into the jumbled rocks below, where I land hard. The shock of the fall is like a slap in the face. After lying quietly for a minute, allowing the pain in my right shoulder and hip to die down, I struggle to my feet. Shaken, I slowly and carefully thread my way through the rest of the rock maze, saving my strength for the battle to come. After an hour and a half I am 800 feet above the parking lot. Our car hasn't moved. Liz is still down there, watching, waiting until she can see me start up the Tower itself.

To my left is the top of a vertical wall dropping hundreds of feet to the beginning of the talus slope. Above this wall, the great overhang soars into the clouds. Between the wall and the overhang, a ledge leads up and left – the Tower Traverse route. The rock is loose and shattered. As I creep along the ledge, the exposure beneath my heels grows quickly. After 100 feet I reach the start of the "real" climbing. It's a relief to be past that rotten section.

I optimistically scan the wall above, but my rising hopes are quickly flattened by reality. A string of bolts creeps up the blank wall. That's encouraging, except for the way they stick out from the rock at crazy angles like the heads and necks of half-witted geese. Good grief! Couldn't they have done a better job than that? Then I remember Macdonald's comments about how tough it was to drill holes in the super-hard rock of the Tower. Even Warren Harding, who drills blank rock with more gusto than anyone, shied away from the brute labor needed to properly set bolts in this extremely dense granite.

As I study the grim ladder leading into the unknown, old doubts, like bubbles in heating water, rise to the surface: Why am I here? What if I break an arm or a leg? What if I have to be rescued?

Rescued... how embarrassing! But there's no help for it. I have to risk both injury and looking the fool if I am to have a chance at getting up this wall. That risk is the spice that flavors the toil. Without danger it would be little more than a lot of hard work.

But it's still a lot of hard work. Being alone, the labor will be huge – and relentless. With a partner, you can at least rest while belaying. But when you're soloing a big wall, you not only lead each pitch, you have to go back down and clean it too. You go over the same ground three times. And then you have to do all the hauling. So why go alone?

You go alone because of what you don't know but want to learn. I know I can climb the Tower with a partner. I only believe I can do it without one. I'm not certain what would happen if I fall. I believe my self-belay will work. I believe my prusiks will hold. More important is what happens in my mind. Am I mentally tough enough? Can I keep my nerve? I believe I can, but there's only one way to find out. I start up.

Growing out of the ledge, a scrawny pine claws its way toward light and life. I climb its flimsy limbs for 15 feet and, with a carabiner, clip my climbing rope into the first gooseneck bolt. I don't like it. If it doesn't hold my weight I'll crash down onto the ledge, probably bounce off, and keep going until the rope stops me. I put a sling around the top of the tree and clip the rope in. Not much better; the tree top is thin and bends easily.

I can imagine the conversation:

"Robbins tried to solo the Tower."

"Tried? How far did he get?"

Letting out from the scrawny tree

"Fifteen feet."

"Hah!"

"Fell. Broke a leg. Had to be rescued."

"Serves him right, trying a stunt like that."

With one foot on a limb and a hand clutching the treetop, I clip an aid sling into the bolt and slip my foot into the sling's lowest rung. I stare at the bolt in fearful anticipation, as I gradually transfer my weight to it. Then I give a few gentle bounces. It holds.

Taking a deep breath, I clip on a second aid sling, step into it, and release my grip on the tree. The bolt still doesn't move. Sloth-like, I creep up the steps of my slings, anxious, dry-mouthed, expecting to be airborne at any moment. With a rush of relief I clip into the second bolt. I feel even safer after clipping into the third one. So it goes, from one bolt to the next, each of them sticking out, crooked and corrupt, threatening instant failure. Rattled, I tell myself: They held Warren, they'll hold you. Then I remember I weigh more than he does.

Slowly entering the realm of the overhang, I am at first amazed that these paltry pieces of twisted metal are holding. But by the time I clip the tenth bolt, dread has been replaced by growing confidence.

My system is working. The 11 mm climbing rope is tied to the bottom of the tree. I am attached to the rope by two prusik knots. These slip knots, made of 5/16 inch rope wrapped around my climbing line, slide easily up the rope but grip tight when weight is applied. Invented for ascending ropes, they're also good – I'm betting – for holding falls. One knot should stop me, but I use two, in case one fails. The prusiks are connected to my swami belt – ten turns of 1

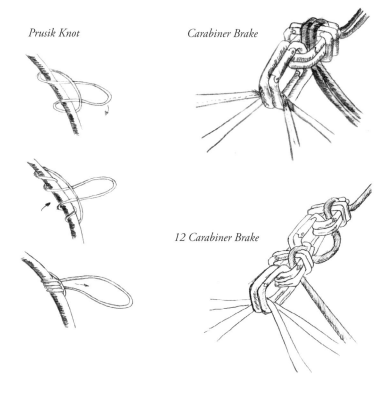

Prusik Knot

Carabiner Brake

12 Carabiner Brake

Drawings by Kirk Visola

inch nylon webbing wrapped around my waist, making a wide band that will cushion a fall much better than would a single loop of rope.

The 9 mm rope is also attached to my waist. It dangles free below me, dropping vertically and then curving back in to the wall, where the other end is anchored to the tree. It will be my link back to the ledge.

I'm now 50 feet above the ledge. If a bolt pops out, I will fall only about 10 feet or so before the elasticity of 50 feet of climbing rope provides the gift of a soft landing – easier on my body and reducing the risk of pulling out more bolts.

Even with this growing security, I still wish Harding had drilled the holes deeper. I readily see, though, why he didn't. Drilling holes is exhausting work at best. It's far worse when you have extra-hard granite like this, and need to stand high in your slings and reach far above your head, leaning backward on an overhanging wall. You have to hit the drill again and again with a heavy hammer, hit and twist, hit and twist, until you're panting and your arms are burning and you want to be down in the meadow below, with a loaf of sourdough, a bottle of wine, and a girlfriend.

Halfway up the first pitch, the bolt ladder abruptly ends, replaced by a thin crack splitting the smooth wall above. I climb this by placing four pitons, one after another. It only lasts for 20 feet, and then the crack disappears and I am again clipping gooseneck bolts for another 30 feet to a hanging belay. Here I am delighted to find two sturdy anchor bolts – 3/8 of an inch in diameter and sunk an inch and a half deep. I find myself thinking of Warren and Glen and Al. Thank God they took the time to place reliable anchors at the belay stations. Of course this is only the top of the first pitch, but I am guessing that it indicates a pattern: marginal, 1/4 inch bolts for climbing, with solid, hefty anchors where they belayed.

After clipping both ropes to these bolts, I rappel the 9 mm rope using 12 carabiners to form a carabiner brake with enough friction to control the rappel. I soon lose contact with the rock and find myself dangling in air. At the bottom I am 20 feet out from the wall. Good thing I tied the end of the 9 mm to the tree. Grasping the rope firmly, I pull myself hand over hand in to the ledge.

Now I'm ready to go back up to collect my gear. Reattaching the prusiks to the climbing rope, I follow the pitch much as I had led it, sliding the protective knots up as I go. As I climb, I remove the carabiners and clip them to my hardware sling, leaving the bolts in place. When I come to the pitons, I hammer them back and forth to loosen them and then add them to the carabiners on the sling around my shoulder.

Arriving again at the top of the first pitch, I clip to the anchors, take a deep breath, and relax. I've now completed Act I of a ten-act performance – one pitch down, nine to go. I turn and look out beyond the overhang to see heavy rain. For hours I've been totally focused on fighting for every vertical foot. I don't know how long it's been raining, but it doesn't matter. Let it rain. The more it rains, the more certain I am this is the place to be.

Turning my attention to the second pitch, I follow another line of bolts 60 feet up orange-brown granite to a 2-foot ceiling. Into a crack in the back of the little overhang I drive a piton straight up. Then, standing as high as possible in my slings, I look for the next placement, but see only pieces of torn metal sticking out of a 1/4 inch hole. This must be where they removed bolt hangers for use on the upper wall.

Alerted by Macdonald's article, I have come prepared. Where entire bolts have been removed there are clean holes. Into these I hammer 1/4 inch Rawl studs, a type of bolt with flanges that compress when driven into a hole in hard rock. They go in less than an inch but are more secure than the expansion bolts they are replacing. Harding's bolts are the sheath type, in which a hammered nail expands the sheath against the side of the hole. In many cases the hole is clogged by remnants of the sheath. Sometimes I am able to dig the scraps out with my hammer, drill, or fingers. Otherwise I just drive a new nail, like the originals, into the wreckage of twisted metal.

Then I clip in an aid sling and slowly apply my weight to the doubtful mess, hoping it will hold. The first test of my self-belay could come at any moment. At one spot I nest two nails together, managing to drive them only 1/4 inch deep. With the hammer I bend the nails up and tie them off with a loop of parachute cord to reduce leverage. Somehow, even this holds my weight.

I'm now moving *very* slowly, trembling, staring, like a mouse at a rattlesnake, at my unlikely improvisations, astonished that they are holding. At last I reach a pair of 3/8 inch anchor bolts and clip in. Despite the cold, I am damp with sweat.

After taking a few minutes to calm down, I scan the nasty pitch I have just finished, aware that, since my rappel rope is fixed on the first pitch, I must now climb back down. I don't want to, but there's no choice. After anchoring my rope I slowly descend, clipping from one uncertain bolt to another, protected by my prusiks. As I reach the bottom of the second pitch I am tempted to continue on down to the ledge. There I can eat and drink and sleep the night away. I can always clean pitch 2 in the morning. I nearly give in, but it's still light, so I push aside soft thoughts and go back up, removing the gear. As I retrieve the carabiners, some of my improvised bolts fall out in my hands.

It's getting dark as I reach the top of the pitch. This first day is about over, but I certainly don't want to spend the night here. The wall is perfectly smooth; there is no hint of a ledge. Leaving my sling of hardware at the anchor, I rappel the second pitch on the 11 mm rope and pull myself back in to the wall at the bottom anchor. I do the same on the first pitch using the fixed 9 mm rope and land back on the ledge where I will spend the night.

Sitting with my back against the tree, I begin pulling bivouac gear from the pack – first a light sweater, then my French down jacket, and finally an anorak to shield me from any stray moisture that might wander in under my "umbrella." Snug and warm, I finally have time to listen to the angry rumblings of my stomach. I break out the food and, as night slowly settles around me, I feast on salami, cheese, bread rolls, and several handfuls of gorp, topping it off with half a quart of water.

By the time I finish, darkness is complete. Peering down over the edge of my eyrie, I watch car lights creeping along the Valley roads. All is quiet. I'm beginning to feel optimistic – satisfied with my progress, confident I can deal with the challenges to come. Looking forward to a good night's rest, I tie myself to the pine, in case I have an urge to walk in my sleep.

I wonder what Liz is doing, and how she is doing. No need to wonder. With poise and grace, she makes everything around her dance to the rhythm of her buoyant spirit. I picture her – radiantly alive. When I get back to the Valley after the Tower she'll be there, waiting. With this soothing thought, I rest my head on a pillow of slings and carabiners, curl up, and fall instantly to sleep.

. . .

At dawn, the temperature has dropped. A light breeze swirls a few snowflakes about the ledge. Out beyond the overhang, snow falls as a thick curtain of white, obscuring the Valley and creating a scene eerie in its beauty and silence. Alone on the Leaning Tower, I'm at peace. A strange sort of peace, perhaps, that looks forward to a daylong struggle up an overhanging wall. Who knows what climbers are made of? Before I start up, though, I need breakfast. It's the same food as the night before – no bacon and eggs up here!

After eating, I stow my gear in the pack, to which I tie the end of the 9 mm rope. Then I set the pack on the ledge next to the tree, wrap two prusik knots around the 9 mm, and start up. At first I go nowhere because my body weight causes the rope to stretch, but soon I am suspended a foot above the ledge. With my weight entirely on the slender line – which seems to have gotten thinner overnight – I use my extra slings doubled around the tree to ease myself off the ledge. But when I am only five feet out, I have to let go of one end.

Suddenly I shoot out into space in a terrifying swing hundreds of feet above the talus. After reaching the farthest point of my arc, I ride the rope back toward the ledge, kissing it briefly with my feet before again careening out over the void. Swinging back and forth, like the pendulum of a grandfather clock, all I can do is hold on and hope to keep my breakfast down. Gradually, the arcs get smaller and smaller, and finally cease. Then, because of twists in the rope, I begin to spin clockwise, seeing first the white curtain of snow, then the dark wall of rock, then snow, then rock, snow, rock....

Dangling in thin air, so far from the wall, my head starts to spin. I've got to get out of here! I begin to climb the rope by standing up in my slings while sliding my chest prusik up. Then, hanging from my chest prusik, I reach down and slide up the prusik holding the slings for my feet. I repeat this maneuver again and again, realizing how much trust we put in these little knots and slings, not to mention this rope only as thick as my pinkie. Did I tie the knot at the top good and tight? I think so. Are those bolts solid? I think so. Is the rope going over any sharp edges? I don't think so, but I'll soon find out. I slide my prusiks up. Gradually the wall comes closer. It's a relief to touch it again.

When I finally arrive at the top of the first pitch, I use the 9 mm to pull up the pack. I get the bag only halfway up before the pain in my arms forces me to throw a hitch on a carabiner. This hauling while standing in slings is more difficult than I expected. I need to rest again before I pull in enough rope to grab the pack with its precious cargo. I attach it to one of the bolt hangers using a special metal hook. The pack will come free when I pull the rope from above. I prusik up the second pitch and haul the pack. It hasn't gotten any lighter. Besides the arm pain, my palms are getting sore from the thin rope cutting into them. This extra wear and tear on my arms and hands may become a serious problem. There must be an easier way! I vow to find it.

Now, at the top of the second pitch, I am seriously committed. With ropes hanging free, far out from the rock below, I can no longer escape by rappelling. To retreat, I would have to climb down, placing pitons and clipping bolts as I did when I came up. It would be necessary to again pass over every pitch three times and again risk bolt failures and falls. Well, forget that! If I climb into trouble, I will have to climb out of it – over the top.

THE THIN EDGE OF THE VOID

God, this is a wild place. Maybe they're right. I must be crazy to be up here alone. But if I can finish this climb, I'll prove I'm not. That won't change their minds. Well, I won't change mine, either.

As I begin the third pitch, the white curtain is turning back into rain, and pieces of the Valley are reappearing far below. I nail good piton cracks to the top of the pitch, where I find the now familiar pair of 3/8 inch bolts. They warm my heart like two old friends.

I anchor the 9 mm line, rappel down it, and pull myself back in to the wall. I'm getting used to this routine, floating around in space as they do in science fiction. But I do it very carefully. One little mistake and I'm gone.

Re-ascending the third pitch, I loosen the pitons by knocking them back and forth, and then remove and clip them to the hardware sling around my shoulder. In my feverish quest for security I have overdriven some of the pitons, and these are beasts to retrieve. But I patiently endure the necessary toil because I will need the pins above.

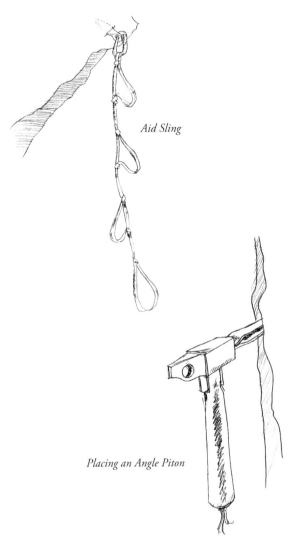

Aid Sling

Placing an Angle Piton

Drawings by Kirk Visola

After breezing up the third pitch, I am slowed to a crawl on the fourth. The cracks are shallow and bottoming – the worst kind. They accept just the tips of my pitons, forcing me to dip into my bag of technical tricks, such as nesting two or three pitons together or tying off the blade next to the rock to reduce leverage.

It's exhausting work, keeping me in a state of high tension. A piton might pop at any time. I hate trusting my weight to these pins, but I have to do it. I tell myself, You've got two prusiks; they can't both fail. Shakily reassured, I continue, climbing farther and farther outward, over the void, as I inch farther up the overhanging wall.

Twice I manage to place a bomb-proof piton by inserting it deeply into a crack and then, swinging away furiously, driving it right up to the eye, to which I eagerly attach a carabiner and my climbing rope. I know I will have trouble getting it back out, but that's a problem for the future. Right now, I want a piton I can trust!

Near the top of the fourth pitch, I step from my aid slings onto a friction slab. Friction slab? I don't remember reading about this. What's a slab doing up here in the realm of the overhang? I climb the slab to reach a small stance, the first ledge on the route. This must be Guano Ledge. Twenty feet to the left is the fabled Ahwahnee Ledge. I easily traverse to it. Reaching Ahwahnee is a major achievement. I am now almost halfway, and I have a secure staging ground for an assault on the upper wall.

After cleaning the fourth pitch and hauling the pack, I'm back at Ahwahnee by mid-afternoon. There's enough time to climb the next pitch before dark.

It's a good thing I have hours to spare, for I immediately get off route. After climbing thirty feet I look up to see smooth, flawless, orange-brown rock. Bolts are the only answer, but there are none. I must be going the wrong way. I give up on this fruitless line and return to Ahwahnee Ledge seeking alternatives. At first, I see none. I keep searching. They had to go somewhere! Then, over beyond Guano Ledge, I spy a corner that might hide a crack. Crossing back to Guano, I move right and chance upon a bolt I had missed earlier in my eagerness to reach Ahwahnee. From the bolt I drop down to the right over a sharp overhang to find a crack marked by faint piton scars. This is it! Back on route, I first nail up and right before following a vertical crack to the top of the pitch. I happily fix my rope to the solid anchors. It's a good high point for today.

Now I just want to get back to Ahwahnee Ledge, to food, water, and luxury accommodations. The rappel rope goes diagonally down and left to its anchor on Guano Ledge. My rappel goes well at first, but soon I am suspended under the overhang at the bottom of a "V" caused by slack in the rope and my weight on it. From this point the rope goes up to Guano, but no one has yet discovered how to rappel *up*. I thrash about, clutching at prusiks and slings, making the awkward transition from rappel to prusik while dangling in space. Finally, gasping and grunting, I emerge from under the overhang and regain Guano Ledge. I cross over to Ahwahnee and collapse in a heap. I've had enough for today. This ledge feels too good. I'll clean that pitch in the morning.

Gazing out from my flat refuge in a tilted world, I see that the rain is changing back to snow. Large white flakes, wafted by a light breeze, drift erratically near the wall. Some of them land on the ledge but, protected by my adversary, I am largely untouched by them.

Adversary? Macdonald, at the end of his account, refers to the Tower as "our huge granite friend."

I don't yet see the Tower as a friend, but this is certainly a friendly ledge, flat and roomy, a classic bivouac spot in the middle of nowhere. The void is still out there, but for now, I don't have to worry about falling into it. I can relax, as if I had stepped into another world. I find myself traveling back through time: my first visit to Yosemite, climbing and arguing with Harding, my decision to try the Tower, talking it over with Liz. Ah, Liz ... where are you now...?

Suddenly I realize it's getting cold and dark. After putting on my down jacket and anorak, I take off my shoes, put on extra socks, and slip my legs into the emptied-out pack. Luxury indeed! I eat, drink, and think about how far I have come.

So far, so good. I have been climbing well and safely and not making mistakes, except for losing my way briefly on the pitch above. It looks as if Liz was right: I can do it. I have spent the entire day swinging around in the middle of an overhanging wall. Dangling over the void, hanging by a thread, I wasn't gripped – except at times. I was, mostly, relaxed and confident. There was a time in my life when such self-assurance in a place like this would have been only a dream.

DISCOVERING MY CALLING

The dream started many years ago. I remember how, as a boy, I chose climbing as a way of life. A book from the Los Angeles Public Library lit the flame. I was 15 years old, wrestling, like many teenagers, with vexing questions that boiled down to "How in the heck do you grow up, anyway?" Wrapped in a cloud of self-centeredness, I couldn't imagine other teens having their own problems. Again and again I catalogued my shortcomings: I couldn't make it socially, got terrible grades in school, and lacked any ability for team sports. I was so at sea I took a perverse pride in my confusion. To be such a failure, I reasoned, I must somehow be above average in something else. I had to be smarter, or more sensitive, or more poetic, or something.

Why, then, I might have asked, were my only friends outcasts like myself? If I was intelligent, why did I get mostly D's and F's? Why did my IQ tests say I was hopelessly average? I might have asked these questions, but I didn't, since my only hope lay in some sort of hidden superiority. But if I had any special talent, it seemed beyond my reach to discover what it was. I was on a downward spiral and beginning to toy with the idea of putting a bullet through my brain. Dimly aware that I needed something bigger than my miserable self to which to devote my miserable self, I began asking what I might become.

The answer had been given a year earlier, when I climbed Fin Dome on a Boy Scout trip to the High Sierra. On that ascent, when I touched the rock, it had in turn touched my spirit, awakening an ineffable longing, as if I had stirred a hidden memory of a previous existence, a happier one. While I was climbing, it was glorious to be alive. Why didn't I then see it as my destiny? Because I was just a kid. I was still too young and simple to comprehend that coping with anything as vast and complex as life requires a terrifying commitment to something larger than one's self. I wasn't about to make such a commitment, not if I could help it. I mean, what if I committed to the wrong thing?

Another year passed, a year of angst and anger and other manifestations of the earthquake of the soul that is a typical teenager's life.

It was a year of vaguely groping for answers to half-formed questions. The questions grew in volume and clarity, demanding answers. But looking to the future, all I could see was a gray fog of nothingness. That was the worst possible thing – to be nothing! I became desperate to fill that void with a picture I could be proud of – a soldier, perhaps, a policeman, a firefighter, a forest ranger – maybe a forest ranger. That was a bit like being a Boy Scout grown up – helping find people lost in the woods, fighting fires, caring for injured animals. I could imagine being a ranger, but I couldn't imagine taking the giant step of devoting my life to it, or to anything else. Again and again I asked the question, What am I going to be?

For a second time I was given the answer. One evening in September 1950, I was reading chapter after spellbinding chapter of *High Conquest*, a history of mountaineering by James Ramsey Ullman. One passage left a deep imprint on the soft clay of my youthful mind:

> *That men have climbed the Matterhorn and McKinley, Aconcagua and Nanda Devi – and that they will eventually climb Everest itself – means little. That they should want to climb them and try to climb them means everything. For it is the ultimate wisdom of the mountains that a man is never more a man than when he is striving for what is beyond his grasp, and that there is no conquest worth the winning save that over his own weakness and ignorance and fear.*
>
> *"Have we vanquished an enemy?" asked Mallory.*
>
> *And there was only one answer:*
>
> *"None but ourselves."*

Photogragh from High Conquest

It is not the summit that matters, but the fight for the summit; not the victory, but the game itself.

"The game itself" – that was the quest for me. I was disgusted with my own "weakness and ignorance and fear." The thought of using climbing to conquer them glowed like the Holy Grail. I could climb and grow strong and brave, and perhaps wiser too.

Turning a few pages I came upon a photograph that completed the conversion from baffled teenager to dedicated mountaineer. The picture showed a climber inching his way up a cliff, clinging to the rock with only fingertips and the toes of his boots. Behind him snowy mountains swept upward, and clouds billowed in the sky. From his waist a rope dropped into space. The caption at the bottom told the story: "Hard rock, thin air, a rope."

That did it. There he was – a man above the abyss. One mistake and he's gone. Yet he's not gripped. He's relaxed, confident, master of the rock. I saw then what I wanted to become. Closing the covers of the book, I realized I had something to live for. I would become that climber in the photo, as I imagined him to be: bold, skillful, fearless. I could, and I would, commit my life to that dream.

The very next day, after school, I hitchhiked 20 miles from my home in Hollywood to the town of Chatsworth, near the western border of the San Fernando Valley. From earlier train-hopping escapades, I knew of a plentiful supply of sandstone outcrops there. These served as whetstones for honing climbing skills. The prize area was Stoney Point, a 300-foot hill girdled by a series of cliffs and crowned with a maze of large, rounded rocks. Boulders were also scattered around the base, providing superb ropeless climbing.

I had climbed here before, but now I returned with a greater sense of purpose. I spent countless hours on these boulders, training for unknown mountains of the future. Here I could safely exceed my abilities, falling off again and again, landing on the forgiving turf. Through this bouldering, which I could do alone when I had no companion, I strengthened my body, improved my technique, grew in confidence, and learned the all-important difference between giving up and giving it my best.

Hitching rides to Stoney Point, along busy streets and freeways from the urban heart of Los Angeles to the rural edge of the Santa Susana Mountains, became a daily ritual. I grew strong on a steady diet of Stoney's sandstone. I had begun a new life, a journey that eventually led, through many twists and turns, to my bivouac here on the Tower.

Now, stretched out on Ahwahnee Ledge, I drift into sleep, at peace with the thought that I have become the climber of those youthful dreams.

CHAPTER II

A Mountaineer Is Always Free

Early years – Royal and puppy

BEGINNINGS

Where did it begin, the trail that led to the Tower? In Point Pleasant, West Virginia, where I was born early in the morning of February 3, 1935. It was a difficult birth. Poor Mom. I almost killed her – a shabby way to treat someone struggling to give you the precious gift of life. Her labors lasted through the night in the small bedroom of our home on the West Virginia side of the Ohio River. A hospital and even a doctor were luxuries beyond my parents' means. Deep in her struggles, writhing in pain, and beginning to despair, Mom heard one of the midwives say "It's a pity she has to die so young."

That remark got Mom's attention. She gritted her teeth, held on, and survived. I was of no help. I wouldn't be born, not if I could avoid it, but fighting proved useless. They drew me kicking and screaming from my room of warmth and security into a cold world of blinding light and ceaseless challenge. The exchange didn't seem to be much of a bargain at the time.

My first three years are lost in the snowdrifts of memory, but Mom recalls how, before I could walk, I went on hands and knees to the screen door, pushed it open, and wandered out onto the front porch. Why not? I had seen many an adult go through that door and return unharmed. Crawling down the porch steps, I was halfway to the end of the block before anyone discovered I was gone. Little did my mother realize this was the inauguration of a pattern of restless seeking and an urge to explore that would try her sweet temper and give her, in the years to come, many a sleepless night.

What was it like, this state where I was born? It began as part of Virginia. Twelve years after the Declaration of Independence, Virginia became our tenth state. Included within its borders were 24,000 square miles that would later become West Virginia. The union of the eastern and western sections of Virginia was flawed from the beginning. The eastern Virginians were a different breed from those who settled in the western mountains. The easterners, who often were farmers, landholders, slave owners, and comparatively wealthy, tended to be cultured men and women of genteel temperament and refined manners. Eight American presidents were born there, including George Washington and Thomas Jefferson.

The Virginians who lived in the west, on the other hand, were typically rugged, independent-minded frontiersmen, often downright ornery, and jealous of their freedom. This passion for liberty is expressed in the motto of West Virginia: *Montani semper liberi*, which translates to "Mountaineers are always free."

I first learned of that proud motto many years later, after I had left West Virginia to grow up in California and after I had become a climber. The ringing declaration refers, of course, to the sort of mountaineer who lives in the mountains rather than one who climbs them. Still, when I discovered, at age 17, the rallying cry of my home state, it seemed powerfully apt. In mountaineering I had discovered a special kind of freedom: freedom from phoniness and having to fit in, freedom from "the madding crowd's ignoble strife." One could rest peacefully under the epitaph *Montani semper liberi*.

Beyond their different temperament, those in the west nursed a grudge over the easterners' advantage in representation in the State Assembly. The easterners' edge here arose from a state law granting voting rights only to landowners, who were more numerous in the east than in the west. Then, as the Civil War approached, the tensions splitting the nation over the question of slavery opened a door through which the westerners bolted. They petitioned the federal government to grant them statehood separate from Virginia. Congress, controlled by the northern states, was sympathetic to their request. Virginia was a slave state, but those living in the west leaned toward the North on this question, and the Union saw the chance to increase its power. In 1863 West Virginia was born.

West Virginia, land of my freedom-loving forebears, is mostly mountains, earning its nickname "the Mountain State." There are farms, humble by Virginia's standards, clinging to hillsides where settlers have heroically cleared the forests. If Virginia's landscape can be described as sunny and generous, West Virginia's is by contrast introspective and brooding.

Perched on a corner of land where the Kanawha River feeds into the Ohio, Point Pleasant is about as far west as the Mountain State gets. To the local Wyandot Indians, it was "tu-endie-wei," the point between two waters.

In November of 1996, I traveled there from California. I had made a similar journey several years earlier, a visit that had stirred something in my soul, something I could not quite grasp, a suppressed memory perhaps, or some sort of wound. If I could just identify that elusive phantom, I might then better understand myself. So

Obelisk in Tu-Endie-Wei Park, W.V. State Parks (WVDNR)
Photo: David Fattalen

Log cabin at Tu-Endie-Wei State Park

I journeyed back to see if, this time, I could evoke that ghost from the past.

A VISIT TO POINT PLEASANT

Flying over the Ohio River toward Charleston, I watch as the terrain below changes from the rolling lowlands of Ohio to the tortuous topography of West Virginia. It is a state of mountains but also of gorges. There are some larger valleys, such as that cut by the Kanawha River, but more characteristic are short, steep canyons. From the air, the earth is distorted into a bewildering array of ravines and dells, slots and trenches: good country for outdoor sports like river running, hunting, fishing, or, in some areas, rock climbing.

As we approach the landing field on the mesa above Charleston, I realize there isn't a lot of room for error. The plane touches down precisely and stops just before the cliff abruptly ending the runway. I leave the plane, rent a car, and drive down the hill through the state capital, then westward along the Kanawha River. West Virginia's largest river is a wide brown flow, a highway for giant barges carrying ore and other commodities up and down the valley. Along the banks are farms flanked by thickly wooded hillsides. I pass a sign that reads, "Keep Us Rural!" To my right is an abandoned billboard with the names "Stan" and "Joe" scrawled in its center. At the confluence with the Ohio River, a rusty steel bridge arcs over the Kanawha. There is a traffic jam, though it is Sunday.

I drive over the bridge and turn off into downtown Point Pleasant. Here and there I see a "For Rent" sign on a shuttered storefront, but otherwise the business district seems clean, vigorous, and healthy. At the State Theater, the marquee features the movie *Romeo and Juliet*. I proceed to the southwestern edge of town, where a small historical park occupies the point of land where the Ohio and Kanawha meet.

The park commemorates a bloody battle fought here over 200 years ago. In the park center a handsome obelisk details that encounter: on October 10, 1774, Colonel Andrew Lewis led 1,100 Virginia militiamen against a like number of Indians under Keigh-tugh-qua, or Cornstalk, chief of the Shawnee. The militia prevailed, losing 50 of their own and killing 200 Indians. The Battle of Point Pleasant became officially known as the First Battle of the Revolution, since the Indians had been incited by British agents.

Nearby stands a giant silver maple, 18 feet in circumference and more than 200 years old. A log cabin functions as a visitor center, and in front of the park is a street paved with red brick.

Leaving the park, I drive through a variety of neighborhoods, noting the general tidiness, the parks and avenues, the schools and hospital, the signs announcing the local service clubs and churches. I stop at a small cemetery and loiter among the tombstones and fresh flowers left on graves of loved ones. Point Pleasant, with its wooden houses, broad front porches, and spacious lawns, strikes me as a quaint but disappearing piece of Americana. The absence of fences and the merging lawns between houses speak of a sense of community and a level of trust that is poignant to one who has grown up in Los Angeles. The homes themselves are modest and unpretentious. In front of many are crèches depicting the events that occurred in Bethlehem 2,000 years ago, reminding me of the approaching Christmas season. Some are of plywood, others merely cheap plastic replicas of the various figures that played their parts in the biblical drama.

The simplicity is touching, strikingly different from my hometown of Modesto, where some neighborhoods have spectacular displays that make them look like mini-versions of Las Vegas. I admit it's fun to put up all those lights, to make a strong, cheerful Christmas statement, but these humble expressions of faith on the lawns of Point Pleasant residents say more to my heart of the Christmas spirit than the brilliant extravaganzas in California.

I get out of the car and wander the neighborhoods, feeling I am looking through a window into the soul of America, or at least into what had been America's soul. What had I lost here? What had I left behind? Strolling the streets prompts an aching in my heart, a yearning, a reaching for something that is in my blood. I can't quite grasp it. It flickers at the edge of memory, plays just beyond consciousness, and slips away.

The people here are friendly. I pay a visit to Louise and Don Stanley. They live in a small, two-story, white wooden house in the north part of town. Louise is my dad's sister. She is about 80 years old. Her eyes are failing, and she has recently been ill. After spending time in the hospital, she is home now, doing reasonably well. Don, formerly a barge pilot on the local rivers and now retired, is taking good care of her.

We exchange small talk for a while, and Louise begins to reminisce. She says my grandfather was a stonemason who had carved his own tombstone. His grave is back in the hills, up dirt roads not passable this time of year. Too bad. In my present mood of searching for my roots I would like to see it.

Louise then describes how hard my grandfather had been on my father – not abusive, but very demanding. She also tells me how

Early photo of Mom (1938)

poorly my father had treated my mom after they were married, and how much everyone loved her. To arrange the marriage, my dad had gone to the courthouse to get a license and then had gotten his cousin, Naomi, to be a witness. He and Mom got married in the living room of the minister's house. After I was born, we lived upstairs in a rented house in downtown Point Pleasant. There was a flood. I got the measles.

She reads a letter from her friend Gladys Burris. Gladys and her son Virgil had gone "to some of the boxing matches Shannon [my dad] fought. He was a good and fearless fighter and a man born about a century late.... The first time I ever saw Shannon, he came by in a rowboat and helped us move from our flooded house. He had been over to see how his sister Winota was getting along. We are all of the same generation – tough and able to take care of ourselves and others if need be. You must remember, they were young men during the great depression. If you've read John Dos Passos' *USA*, you know what people had to do. They traveled all over the US. Not too much north, but south and southwest, riding the rails, looking for work. Some of their adventures were pretty scary."

Sitting there listening, I have an inkling of what I had missed. I have a vague sense there was once something different in my life, and I have lost it forever. Part of me has always been here, in Point Pleasant. It is as if something had been amputated, and I had been made less whole without realizing it. A feeling of something precious, once real and now gone, sweeps over me. I want to stay and talk, but it is time to move on. I take my leave and drive off, faintly conscious of leaving something behind. Dad, Dad, Dad, why did you do this to me?

Shannon (Royal's Dad) in the Army

MOM MEETS DAD

My mother's family, the Bowens, were a mixture of German, Irish, English, and Scottish ancestry. Mom grew up in Gallipolis, Ohio, just across the Ohio River from Point Pleasant. As a child of seven years, she had a terrible experience. Standing in front of a gas heater, her dress caught fire. The conflagration engulfed her entire body. She nearly died. She has borne the scars, thankfully hidden in normal attire, ever since.

Mom was very beautiful as a young woman, radiant in her purity and innocence. She worked in the lingerie section of a department store in Gallipolis. One day Royal Shannon Robbins came in, looking for "something for his girlfriend." My mother tried to help him, but Shannon, after taking up her time, left without a purchase. He returned again and again, ostensibly for the same purpose, but never bought anything for that girlfriend. Eventually he asked Mom out, and they began dating.

They were married, after a brief courtship, on April 4, 1934. Dad was mostly Irish. Although his name, which he would give to me, was Royal Shannon Robbins, everyone knew him as Shannon. He would always be a mystery to me.

A BRIEF MARRIAGE

My father was a sportsman. He hunted dangerous Alaskan brown bears. While in the Army, he was shipwrecked in Alaska and lay on a beach unable to move for several days before he was discovered and nursed back to health. He wrote up some of his experiences for magazines, though I don't know whether any were ever published. I'm sure he'd read Jack London and Ernest Hemingway and pictured himself following in their footsteps – a romantic adventurer, masculine but sensitive, able to capture his adventures and life for the printed page. He certainly had a talent for fiction, telling Mom many lies, including a whopper he told during their courtship about how he and his twin brother had been in a street fight with a couple of toughs. His brother had been killed, but Shannon had avenged him by slaying the other two combatants. After they were married, Mom was startled to learn from her mother-in-law that Shannon never had a twin brother!

Dad was once the welterweight boxing champion of West Virginia and had played baseball in the minor leagues. He was also Clark Gable handsome. His good looks, breezy self-confidence, physical abilities, and winning ways charmed the ladies. After marrying my mother, he pursued other women, breaking Mom's heart. As his affairs became more flagrant, my mother's resistance grew. Once, after she had followed him to a dance and embarrassed him in front of one of his girlfriends, he came home and trashed all of her clothes, apparently so she couldn't again leave the house and trail him. Though in his anger and frustration he would do violence to inanimate objects, he never physically mistreated Mom or me.

Nevertheless, the marriage soon shattered on the rocks of my father's selfishness. He was neither "husband" to Mom nor "father" to me. Convinced that boys need dads, Mom reluctantly came to the heartsick conclusion that the love of her life must no longer be part of her life. She had been in love – totally, joyfully, foolishly in love – with this dashing, handsome charmer. She probably would love him forever. Now she had to leave him, to find a father for her son. She hired an attorney and began the legal formalities of suing for divorce. I didn't know the word "divorce" at age three but I have come to hate it. Love must not fail. Somewhere along the way I made a vow that, when I got married, it would be forever.

I don't remember anything about the split-up. I probably closed my heart and mind to the pain. Dad must have been a big part of the world to me then, and the rupture revealed what the world was really like. How could my dad leave me? I must have been to blame. There was something wrong with *me*, and that was why Dad left. All my mother's love, which was deep and never ending, was not enough, over the years, to cancel out that first wounding realization of betrayal and loss.

NEW TROUBLES

Mom soon remarried. Her new husband was James Chandler, a machinist from across the Ohio River. He lived in Mansfield and quickly proved a bizarre character. He began family life by changing my name to his. I became Jimmy Chandler. His name was good enough for him, so it would be good enough for me. He would have no high-falutin "Royal." I was to be *his* son. I don't remember any of this. I may have known, more or less, what was going on at the time, but as far as I can remember I knew James Chandler as my real father. Only years later, when he was gone, would Mom allow me to take back my original name.

It was the late 1930s. With the nation still in the grip of the Great Depression, Jim had trouble finding work. His drinking and

Royal and young girl dressed up

disorderly habits led to losing what jobs he did get. As a cosmetician in a local drugstore, Mom became the breadwinner while Jim stayed home and took care of me, more or less. He continued to drink heavily. One evening Mom came home and found that Jim had beaten me savagely, my bottom almost bleeding from the blows.

I had asked for it. Beatings were something I hadn't experienced, so I clumsily walked into trouble. After he said to me, "It's time to go to bed." I asserted myself: "No, I won't do it. You can't make me." Then I thrust in the knife, saying with great intensity, "You're not my *real* father." That put him in a rage. "Oh yeah, I'll teach you who your father is, and you'll never say that to me again." Suddenly, for the first time in my life, I was afraid. He removed his belt, doubled it, took down my pants and laid into me. I learned quickly what real pain was. And he was right. I never again claimed he wasn't my real father. In fact, from then on I thought of him as dad. My real father was erased from my memory. Jim had a streak of domestic violence in him that Shannon was above.

CURIOSITY

Having concluded that Jim wasn't a reliable babysitter, Mom placed me with church women who boarded and cared for children. They were located in the countryside near our home in Mansfield. I don't remember my parents divorcing, and I don't remember Jim beating me, but I do remember being with a girl about my age down in the basement of the foster home we lived in. Being a curious five-year-old, I offered her an exchange: "I'll show you mine if you'll show me yours!" That seemed reasonable enough. Scandalized, she jumped up and raced off to inform the matrons of my attempt at fair trade. They let me know, not in a harsh way, but in a firm one, that what I had done was *naughty*. It was a "bad dog" sort of thing. It was a while before I made an offer like that again.

Two years passed before my faith in little girls was restored. A young lady and I were sitting together on a low wall separating the sidewalk from a tilted grass lawn. We were both dressed up for Sunday school. She wore a little pink dress with white stockings and a pink bonnet. We were chatting innocently when suddenly she reached over and planted a smacker right on my cheek! That was all – a total surprise, remembered with pleasure to this day. I sought that little girl, or someone like her, for many years, finally finding her in the woman who would be my wife.

Another experience in the foster home is seared in my memory: As punishment for wetting my bed, I was repeatedly held under a cold shower by one of the stout ladies who ran the home. She would hold my face up to the full blast of the shower, and though I struggled and struggled, it went on and on. You would think it would have been effective training, but unfortunately for me, and my bed, it didn't work. This may have been another example of an inclination, perhaps part of my Mountain State heritage, to resist authority, to not do what I was supposed to do because I was supposed to do it. So I had to endure the water torture again and again.

Then the matrons had the bright idea of setting an alarm clock next to my bed. It would go off in the middle of the night and wake me up so I could use the toilet. I slept right through the ringing. I never heard it. This annoyed them even more. One can understand their frustration. They had to wash my bedclothes every day! The poor ladies may have been fighting a more persistent demon than they realized. The best moments of my life had been as an infant – warm, cuddled, loved, fed – and I didn't have to wake up to go to the bathroom! Babies do it in bed, so I was probably trying to get back to nirvana by peeing my way there. It didn't work. So far, I wasn't much of a credit to my family.

MOVING WEST

By 1941, as the nation geared up for World War II, news had reached Ohio that machinists were in demand in the defense industries on the west coast. The three of us packed up and drove to southern California where we rented a house in Hermosa Beach. Jim got a job right away but soon lost it. Luckily for him, the need for machinists grew with the approach of war. He was able to move from job to job in spite of excessive drinking and lack of self-discipline. That year he worked at 13 different jobs. In September of 1941 Mom gave birth to my sister, Helen.

It wasn't far from our home to the water and it drew me like a magnet. Neither West Virginia nor Ohio had anything like the mighty ocean that started at the edge of the sand and went on forever. A narrow line of giant boulders arced from the shore into the sea, forming a cove of quiet water for swimmers and moored boats. This was the breakwater. My six-year-old imagination responded to the call of this thin path of big stones leading into the ocean. I ventured forth.

Clambering over the rocks, I soon left land far behind. My only companions were crabs lurking in nooks, hiding in crannies, or sidling across the jumbled rocks. I was surrounded by the roar and splash of the waves as they threatened to snatch me into the mystery of the deep, unfathomable ocean. I loved the tumult, the waves breaking, and the glistening foam. I would sit on the breakwater for hours and watch the surf dash against the rocks, with ceaseless splash of white foam and dreadful sucking menace. I was captivated by the mystery and danger, especially as I could not yet swim.

DREAMS

During this period, when we were living by the beach, I had recurring nightmares. In one of these, an alarm clock sat on a nightstand, ticking, ticking. An air of foreboding filled the room, as if something terrible was about to happen. Suddenly the walls broke in, collapsing on the clock and, presumably, the clock watcher. Was it the Mansfield alarm clock that had failed to wake me in the middle of the night? Did the collapsing walls take the place of showers? Was the foster home experience still with me?

Another dream occurred only once, but I will remember it all my life. I was seven or eight years old, sleeping soundly and blissfully. In my mind's eye I saw my mother being attacked by a giant gorilla. This vision was probably a result of watching *Nyoka, the Jungle Girl* serials at our local movie theater. I was intrigued by Nyoka and her short shorts even at that early age. The dream was so realistic I woke up to find myself ringing our neighbor's doorbell to get help. They were so impressed with my story they called the police. Of course there was no gorilla. Mom and Jim were still sleeping soundly when the police arrived. It was quite a night. The experience foreshadowed a similar episode that would occur a few years later, one that would not be fantastical and would, in a very real and terrifying way, involve my stepfather.

FLYING

I also dreamed of flying – a hopeful contrast to the nightmares. In these dreams I began on the ground, looking up at the sky, wishing I could fly. The wishing turned to fierce desire and then to steely determination as I started flapping my arms, harder and harder, stronger and stronger, until I began to rise off the ground. And there I was, actually a foot above the earth, in the air! Buoyed by this slight success, I flapped even harder and got higher and higher, until I was finally up there, really flying, far above the ground, so far up that I stopped flapping and just glided along. It was like being in heaven, just soaring effortlessly, far above the earth. No wonder we think of birds as free. Being earthbound, by comparison, is like being in prison.

Eventually, realizing I was losing altitude, I renewed my bird-like flapping and, regaining height, got back to where I could again switch to gliding mode. The dream was so vivid I was certain it was real. Looking down, I could see houses here, trees there, and rivers, and roads.... I was truly flying! Then, later, when I awoke, I would remember my dream and realize it had been, after all, just a dream.

Still, compared to reality, I preferred my flying dreams. Fortunately, they kept recurring, as real as ever. Sometimes they began in what seemed like a public library, in the aisles between the stacks of books. I would start flapping my arms furiously, rising off the floor, and then flying up and down the aisles and around the bookshelves. Then I was above the bookshelves, just below the domed ceiling, before darting into the next room where I flapped over the heads of people sitting at tables poring over books. They didn't notice me flying above their heads. Picking up speed and power, I flew out of the building, out and up, above the countryside once again, aloft and free.

Friends have described their flying dreams as joyful soaring, without struggle. My dream-flying, however, could occur only by dint of great effort. I flew not by grace or skill, but by pure force of will. I flew because I *would*. Now, looking back over many wasted years feeling sorry for myself, eating my heart out, cursing God for my lack of grace, talent, or ability to do what others could do, I realize I just didn't get the message. It was all there in my dreams: Any success I would achieve would be through spiritual effort, courage, and pluck, rather than talent. I didn't yet understand that perseverance is a gift too.

I had those flying dreams for years. When did they stop? Where did they go? They disappeared when I got out into the streets of Los Angeles, seeking *real* adventure.

READING

Why did some of the flying dreams occur in libraries? Perhaps even at that early age I sensed that books would help me fly. In books I found heroes, wisdom, and beauty, better worlds than the one surrounding me in Los Angeles.

I devoured books about animals, especially dogs. I read every dog book written by Albert Payson Terhune. I still remember some of the titles: *Lad: A Dog*, *Lochinvar Luck*, *Bruce*, *Gray Dawn*. He wrote mostly about collies, so of course I became convinced that collies were the bravest, most lovable dogs in the world. Terhune wrote in the heroic mode about heroic dogs. Reading his stories about these noble canines, it seemed good to be a hero, even if it meant death, as with Bruce, who died saving a youngster's life. I looked for other dog books and stumbled upon one about three animals, a dog, a cat, and – what? – I can't remember the other creature. They traveled together in the far Northland on some marvelous quest.

I read horse books as well, including *Black Beauty* and *My Friend Flicka*. Then, of course, there was *Bambi*, by the Austrian author Felix Salten, and Seton's *The Life of a Grizzly*. I loved animal books because animals always seemed better than humans – courageous, selfless, and generous. After the animal stories, my next reading passion was the *Hardy Boys*, a series of books of mystery and adventure involving two teenage brothers who fought crime. These siblings, Frank and Joe, were smart, resourceful, and witty, and they always caught the bad guys in the end. Wanting to identify with these winners, I escaped into novel after novel of these youthful heroes.

TRAILER PARK

After a couple of years, we left Hermosa Beach and moved into a trailer park in nearby Redondo Beach. There we lived in a small trailer, all we could afford on Jim's intermittent income. Soon after we moved there, I stepped out of the trailer and was hit in the back by a pellet shot from a BB gun. Some kid in the park was using the new arrival for target practice. I wasn't injured, but it really hurt – as much emotionally as physically. Why would anyone do such a thing? I was discovering that danger lurked in the city.

Soon after that, I nearly lost an eye. I had made friends with a boy from a trailer next to ours. He didn't have a BB gun, but he did own a bow and arrow set, which we took to a nearby vacant lot where we practiced shooting arrows at signs. I thought it would be fun to hide behind a sign when he was shooting at it. I reasoned I would be safe, though deliciously close to danger. So I crouched behind the target sign, waiting for him to shoot. I waited and waited, until I finally began to think, Well, maybe he isn't going to do it. Besides, even if I did stand up, there was little chance he would shoot right then, and even if he did, would he hit me? A pretty small risk. It was chicken not to stand up and see what was going on. Goaded by misguided ideas of courage, I peeped over the top of the sign. Unfortunately, the arrow was just then winging my way. It flew over its target and hit me just above my nose, a 1/2 inch from my left eye. The wooden arrowhead cut the skin, and blood flowed down my face and into my mouth. I was very frightened but not seriously hurt. Money was scarce, so my parents didn't have the wound sutured. For that reason, I bear a slight scar to this day. This was an early example of a tendency to push my luck and take risks. I got away with it. Just barely. It was a good lesson, or it should have been.

SEWARD STREET

When I was nine years old and my sister, Helen, was three, our family left the trailer and moved to Culver City, one of the many smaller towns surrounding the big city of Los Angeles. After living in Culver City for a year and a half, we moved again, this time to Hollywood, then in its heyday as the land of celluloid enchantment.

In a low-income neighborhood one mile south of Hollywood Boulevard, we began life anew in a modest but decent rental at 812 North Seward Street. Directly across from us, to the west, sat a fire station, with a big red engine kept shiny and sparkling by those indefatigable polishers, the firemen. Just south of us was a vacant lot forming a corner at Waring Avenue. Six blocks north, Seward Street crossed Santa Monica Boulevard. In the summer, my friends and I would walk to the boulevard and then hitchhike 20 miles to Santa Monica Beach where we would spend the day bodysurfing and sunning on the sand. Those were carefree days.

We played war games, cowboys and Indians, kick the can, and hide and seek. Once, attempting to hide by crawling through deep grass, I cut my wrist on a piece of broken glass. I still bear the scar. We enjoyed dirt clod fights in our nearby vacant lot, pulling handfuls of tall grass and hurling them at each other. How we loved vacant lots! I had a bicycle collision with a friend at 20 miles an hour when we met at right angles from either side of a blind fence. We survived with minor scratches but the bicycles were a total loss.

One of our ways of passing time was to wander through backyards for the six-block journey to Santa Monica Boulevard. It took longer to get where we were going, but who needed a sidewalk when

Mom at Seward Street (circa 1943)

you could climb through backyards? This habit of avoiding the easy path would later take the form of climbing mountains by the hardest ridge or face rather than up the normal route. The point was not to reach the top of the mountain, nor to get to Santa Monica Boulevard, but to make the journey *interesting*.

One wonders, looking back, how we were able to get away with cutting through those yards. It was certainly a simpler time, when kids wandering through your backyard were assumed to be looking for fun, or mischief at worst, rather than intent on criminal activity. We often went barefoot, which once resulted in the horrible experience of stepping on a rusty nail that went deeply into my foot.

The firemen played horseshoes in an open area just south of the station. Late one afternoon I crossed the street to watch the game and was surprised and delighted when they invited me to join in. They generously overlooked my weak arm and lack of skill, and soon I was feeling as though I was one of them. They always treated me kindly, though I must have been a pest at times. These were my adult role models, and I wanted to be like them – strong, generous, brave, able to joke and laugh and to take life lightly.

With my mother's encouragement, I joined the Cub Scouts. Proudly wearing my dark blue Cub Scout uniform, I strolled over to the house of a girl with whom I was secretly in love. There I spent hours bouncing a basketball off a building across the street from her house, hoping she was watching through a window, admiring my athletic skill and my new role as Cub Scout. I never saw any evidence that my performance captured her fancy.

Unfortunately, life as a Cub Scout was like sand on the campfire of my heart, smothering the incipient flames of adventure. I smol-

My sister Helen (Penny)

dered for a year under the weight of den meetings, mottoes, and pledges. Needing more wildness than my Cub pack could provide, I dropped out. I didn't suspect at the time that a few years later a deeper, more meaningful Scouting experience would enrich my life.

THE DECLINE OF JAMES CHANDLER

Jim and I drifted farther apart. Although nominally father and son, we often came and went like ships passing in the fog, unaware of each other's presence. He didn't mistreat me after we moved to California; he just never seemed to "be there." He came and went. He worked, off and on. He drank a lot. He argued with my mother, sometimes violently. Although I still viewed him as my father, for me he hardly existed. We never did anything as a family. We never went anywhere together. Jim ignored me, and I pretty much ignored him – other than to vow I would never be like him.

One day, when Mom, Jim, and I were hanging around in our front yard, a girl my age from a house down the street stopped by to say hello. Jim suggested I race the young lady to the corner. That sounded good to me. She was slender and looked fit, but after all, she was just a girl. I was sure to win. So, when Jim said "Go!" we ran, and ... she got there first! But what made it worse, unbearable even, was that Jim mocked me for letting a girl beat me. In fact, he called me a sissy. Tears burst from my eyes. Mom tried to comfort me, but it was a terrible moment – the worst thing in my life – being called a sissy!

Then, in a flash of insight, I realized that Jim was not on my side. He enjoyed my defeat. I guess he never would forgive me for being unlike him. I *was* unlike him. I was better, but I didn't dare say so.

Jim & Penny (circa 1943)

I couldn't challenge him, but I could hold him in contempt. That was my revenge. This incident fed a growing conviction that, to be admired and loved, I would have to excel.

Sometimes when Jim was late coming home, Mom would send me to get him. I always knew where to look – six blocks north on Seward and two blocks east on Santa Monica Boulevard, at a bar named Davy Jones' Locker. There I would find him, again and again, elbows on the bar, staring blankly ahead, his mind on his sorrows, banishing his shortcomings with bottle after bottle of Pabst Blue Ribbon. Sometimes we would walk home together. Sometimes he would send me away, saying, "I'll be right there." Sometimes he would come and sometimes he wouldn't.

He sank lower, drinking more and losing job after job. He grew more violent toward Mom, knocking her around, giving her black eyes, hitting her in the stomach. I hated him, but there was nothing I could do except despise him all the more. I tried to ignore it all, reading books and dreaming about flying.

CHAPTER III

Early Adventures

My stepfather sank deeper into his personal hell. He and Mom argued longer and louder, and in their fights Jim's voice now carried a new menace, a promise of more savage violence. With Mom working to help support the family, Jim would come in and ask for money "to pay someone back." It was drinking money, of course, and Mom resisted as much as she dared.

One night, after I had gone to bed, I heard them through the wall of my bedroom, Jim angrily shouting, Mom urgently pleading. I tried to block it out, but I couldn't ignore the chairs hitting the floor as Mom shoved and pulled the table to protect herself. Suddenly Jim harshly commanded, "Come here!" Mom screamed, "Jim, put down that knife!"

Knife! I thought, I've got to get help! Springing from bed, I slipped to the window, silently raised it, and hopped out, running barefoot in my pajamas down the street half a block to the Technicolor plant. The night watchman, seeing my distress, opened the gate enough for me to squeeze through. Once inside the lot, I raised pleading eyes and breathlessly blurted out, "My dad is trying to kill my mom!" He grabbed the telephone and called the police.

Mom later told me how, as I was on my rescue mission, she had fled the house with Jim in hot pursuit. They tore across the lawn, Jim grabbing her jacket just as she stepped off the curb. He had her! Spinning, she left the coat in his hands and darted across the street, frantically knocking on the firehouse door. Jim hesitated and went back into the house. Ten minutes later the police picked me up at the Technicolor plant. We drove the short distance to our house and they went in, leaving me in the patrol car. Mom was OK, and Jim, who had discovered that I had gone for help, had escaped over the back fence.

That was it. Mom had had enough. She filed for divorce. Now it was Mom, Helen, and me. No dad, not even a stepfather.

NAMING MYSELF

With Jim no longer a part of our lives, Mom let me in on the little secret of my real father's identity. She was lying in bed and asked me to come in and sit beside her. "Son, there's something you must know." I wondered why she called me "son" instead of "Jimmy." She explained that, when I was born, I was named Royal Shannon Robbins, after my father. My stepfather had changed my name. My real father was a different sort of man. He had loved her, and she would probably always love him. He had been a boxer and a big-game hunter. He'd played professional baseball, was a writer, and was as handsome as a movie star. I was relieved and happy to learn that Jim wasn't my real father, that my real father was better. Then Mom gave me a tremendous gift. She told me I could change my name back to the original. To change your name at age ten was a big deal, but I didn't hesitate. I instantly knew I wanted to be like my real father. I didn't want my stepfather's name. I could shed it as a snake sloughs its skin. I would become Royal Shannon Robbins.

I expected my new name would give me an elevated status at school, but the immediate effect was schoolmates teasing me. Then and later I would have to endure a lot of jokes about Royal Pudding and other brand names such as Royal Crown Cola. I didn't really mind this. It was done in good humor and was, after all, a kind of attention.

GOODBYE TO JIM

Mom was now keenly aware that husbands and fathers could come and go. She also knew that pure chance might snatch her away at any moment, leaving Helen and me alone in a dangerous world. For our own protection, using trust and encouragement, she worked to build in us the quality of self-reliance. In my case, one way of doing this was allowing me to choose my name. That helped me see I was in charge of my life. Mom always set a frontier example of independence, being resilient and thoroughly self-reliant herself. From her I learned that my troubles were not to be blamed on fate or luck or other people but were of my own making. She helped me see that if there was a mess, I was probably the cause, and I could be the cure.

The idea that we are in charge of our destiny is a deeply optimistic one. This expectation of success, which my mother encouraged, led to a habit of trying new things. Many of these attempts were failures, but some were successes. I learned that failure is never fatal. You can always try again. The only unforgivable thing is giving up. The truly disgraceful thing is being a quitter.

With Mom working six days a week, I was on my own much of the time. I prepared my breakfasts, usually eggs with fried Spam. I packed my lunches, and when I came home from school the first thing I did was kick the trash bin. A mouse or two would often spring out, to be quickly dispatched by our mongrel, Roger. Then I would make myself a giant hamburger sandwich with lettuce and tomato, salt and pepper, mustard and catsup, and heaps of relish. After my snack I usually went out searching for friends to play with until it got dark.

On one such afternoon, as I was enjoying my hamburger, Jim walked through the door into our living room. Oh, no, I thought, instantly on the alert. There was no telling what dark mood might be gripping him. Maybe he wanted to pay me back for bringing the cops. His manner, however, oozed friendliness. He assured me he bore no ill will because I had gone for the police. He would never again hurt my mother, or me, or Helen. He insisted he loved us so much that he would cut off a finger to prove it if I wanted him to do so, pulling out a knife in case I assented. I quickly assured him that wouldn't be necessary. Looking back, the apparent willingness to mutilate himself to prove his love seems mad and sentimental, but poor Jim probably really meant it. In his heart of hearts, he wanted to be good.

After more talk, he got up heavily and stalked out. I was relieved to see him go. You never knew about Jim. As my anxiety faded, it was replaced by a mixture of contempt and pity. James Chandler, a slave to his vile habits, was a desperately unhappy man who hated himself and didn't know what to do about it. That was the last I saw of him. He moved to Venice, on the edge of the Pacific, where he sold vacuum cleaners. There he lived the short remainder of his life, dying in a barroom brawl.

STRIKING OUT ON MY OWN

A few months after Jim left, I ran away from home. Running away is the weapon kids use to repay the adult world for real or imagined offenses. It gets the big folks' attention and, by their reaction, measures the youngsters' importance. It was my grandmother's fault (I was not about to accept blame for anything). She was living with us at the time, helping Mom in Jim's absence. She was a big woman, accustomed to being obeyed. I had broken some rule, I don't know which one, and she was intent on punishing me. I would have obeyed Mom, but I wasn't having any of my grandmother's dictatorship. I ran into the street with grandma on my heels. She tried to snag me, but I was too fast. Realizing my power to defy adults would be short-lived when Mom came home and they got together, I ran down the street and around the corner, out of sight of grandma and her tyranny.

I slept under a hedge that first night, as Mom roamed the streets, calling, "Royal!" "Royal!" Part of me, hearing my new name, desperately wanted to go out and throw myself into her arms. Another part wanted to "teach her a lesson," whatever that might have meant to my imperfectly developed moral sense. I stayed hidden under the hedge.

Over the next several days, I lived in a Salvation Army warehouse. There I found blankets, furniture, games, and comic books! The comics were an unexpected treat, and I read dozens and dozens. For a young boy, stumbling upon an endless supply of comic books was like discovering gold. During the day, when the men were working there, I hid behind the furniture, relishing my newfound freedom. I don't remember what I ate, but I must have found something. The novelty, intoxicating at first, wore off after four days and I returned home. Like the prodigal son, I was welcomed back and forgiven.

YMCA CAMP

My buddies and I passed many hours in the big swimming pool at the YMCA. This was back in the days of polio, and we were aware that the dread disease could be spread in public pools. The danger and the fear were real, but, in our minds, the fun of the pool outweighed the risk of the crippling disease. The Young Men's Christian Association provided numerous other activities to keep us kids out of trouble. Besides swimming, we played basketball, handball, and checkers, and I learned the more challenging game of chess. But the biggest gift from the "Y" was my first outdoor experience. YMCA camp was the highlight of my young life. We spent a week living out of tents, exploring, treasure hunting, building campfires, singing, and hiking.

Camp was a raucous affair, filled with laughing and shouting, but the noise was beautiful – the loud joy of life. Back in the city I was always trying to be something I wasn't – cool, sophisticated, smart, or whatever – always trying to fit in. Out here I could just be myself. The outdoors seemed to be in my blood. I wrote a brief letter to my mother:

> *Dear Momy, I am having a lot of fun here at camp and the days go very slow here. that's what is good about it. this is only my second day her and it seems like I have been here for a week. I sent daddy a card tallying him that I am here. when I*

got here I had to lug the suitcase up 50 dert stares of dirt. it is
a vary coxing [cozy] littel cabin and there is 7 other kids in it.
we each have our own kot. tomorrow we have archery. it is rite
after noon now. well that's all I have to say now. I well rite you
a letter in five days.

> *Roual jr. xxxxxxxxxxx*
> *ps...don't forget to write*

AT SCHOOL

I attended Vine Street Elementary School, located on the west side of Vine Street ten blocks south of Hollywood Boulevard. From my home at Seward and Waring it was a six-block walk to the school, a typical two-story institutional building with a big gravel recreation area and a few oak trees with thick, soft, corky bark. I hated studies but loved schoolyard games. My favorite was dodge ball: A group of kids stood inside a circle some 20 feet across, while others lined the perimeter and tried to hit those inside with a large ball. If touched by the thrown ball you were out. The winner was the last boy or girl left in the circle. Being fast and agile, I excelled at dodge ball and often was the last one standing.

In contrast to the joy of the playground, classes were depressingly difficult. Except for reading, which I liked, everything else in English class was maddeningly obscure, especially the parts of speech and diagramming sentences. I would try my best, or what I thought was my best, but I just couldn't get it. Arithmetic was worse. I found numbers even more mysterious than words. Lacking an academic fighting spirit, I would take my homework to Mom and whine and whimper about how hard it was, hoping she would somehow transform me with a few encouraging words into someone who could do the arithmetic. She said the words and tried to encourage me, but my perversity wasn't going to let her get between me and the delicious conviction that I was hopeless. I began to develop a picture of myself as a loser at school. Why was I so stupid? Why was everyone else so smart? God, why did you make me this way?

This habit of looking for the worst in myself led to poor citizenship in the classroom. I began to be sent to the principal's office for various offenses, such as tormenting one teacher who was so sweet and gentle that I knew I could get away with outrageous behavior. When I was talking in class or throwing paper airplanes, she used to plead across the room, again and again, "Royal, leave it off. I tell you, Royal, leave it off!" My vilest act was starting a fire in the wastebasket in her room. I shudder to think about it now. I should have been disciplined with a rod, but there were no rods. I didn't have a dad who would say to me, "You just don't do that!" So I pushed and pushed, doing more and more outlandish things, unconsciously trying to find that line that must not be crossed.

When I was in the fifth grade, a new student arrived at Vine Street Elementary. His name was Royal Slagle. I had never met another Royal. Slagle was friendly and surprisingly generous. I had barely introduced myself when he asked me if I would like to borrow his bicycle. Borrow his bicycle? Of course! I hadn't been on a bike since wrecking mine in that collision a year earlier. Slagle was slight and wiry, a fast runner, quick, and deft of movement. He liked to get out and take risks as much as I did. He was from lower-class Irish stock and lived only a few blocks from my home in Hollywood. We became best friends.

Another new friend was Steve Smith. Steve was a blond, freckle-faced kid, also from the lower stratum of society. We three stuck together and had many adventures.

A third buddy, Thomas Ackawie, was not really part of our intimate group and was less likely to get into trouble than Steve, Royal, and I were. Nevertheless, Tom and I went through backyards together and roamed the streets of Los Angeles. We got a kick out of riding the big red streetcars down Hollywood Boulevard. Often hooked together, the cars operated on steel tracks and were powered by electric cables strung overhead. A short ride was 6 cents, but we could go all the way to Santa Monica Beach for 15 cents. Of course 15 cents each way is 30 cents total, and that cut seriously into our movie money. That's why we hitchhiked so often.

The fantasy world of the Silver Screen had us firmly in its grip. Most of our money was spent on Saturday afternoons at the Hitching Post, a theater on Hollywood Boulevard specializing in western films. It was our church and those movies were our weekly spiritual food. The good guys, like Tom Mix and Roy Rogers, always won, and the endings were never sad. The sense of authenticity was heightened by the requirement that we check our toy guns and cap pistols at the door. Movies were 10 cents. A bag of popcorn, a necessity, cost five more precious pennies.

This was in 1945, at the end of World War II, when a coin found lying in the gutter meant you were having a lucky day. Many commodities were rationed, enabling us to earn money by collecting things like coat hangers, newspapers, and bacon grease. This last item we acquired by going from house to house with gallon buckets, later selling the grease for a penny a pound. We also collected aluminum foil, mostly from cigarette wrappers. We scrounged these wherever we could find them – on sidewalks, in gutters, under seats in diners. The very scarcity of these items made them valuable and therefore worthy targets for young scavengers with plenty of time and no money.

When I last saw Tom Ackawie he was an artist in Berkeley, California, where he worked out of the same studio on University Avenue for more than 35 years.

IDYLLIC SUMMERS

Between the ages of 10 and 12, my friends and I passed nearly every day from June through August at Santa Monica Beach. Each summer morning we – sometimes Steve and Royal and I, sometimes Tom and I – thumbed rides 20 miles to the ocean, where we played all day in a world of sun, surf, and sand. Even on very warm days the ocean itself was shockingly cold. Yet we braved the waters again and again, staying in as long as we could bear the chill before emerging shivering to throw ourselves face down on the hot sand. After a few minutes soaking up the delicious warmth, we rolled over onto our backs, becoming encased in a protective coat of sand that by and by dried and fell off, leaving us warm and ready to challenge the breakers anew.

Bodysurfing was our first choice of ocean games, though rarely did we ride a wave gracefully from surge to shore. Instead of riding, it was more like churning, with the waves tumbling us about willy-nilly, like rats in a Maytag. Often, in the foamy aftermath of a giant wave that had spun me upside down, I fought the swirling water, eyes open to seek the sunlight, lungs desperate for air, finally breaking the foam to gulp mouthfuls of lifesaving oxygen. Years later, when something went wrong in whitewater kayaking, I would repeat these desperate struggles.

The hazards of the ocean were a key part of the experience. We heard much of the threat of "undertow," and were ever alert to it, though we never were actually towed under. We loved the feeling of danger, riding big waves or swimming farther and farther from shore, wondering what fearsome creatures were lurking beneath our legs. We took the jellyfish alerts seriously. Lifeguards posted signs warning of Portuguese man-of-war jellyfish, whose sting was extremely painful as well as, we were told, paralyzing. We were lucky never to be stung, but nothing could keep us from the ocean. A shark attack might have, but in those days we never heard of one happening in those waters.

The beach was separated from the town of Santa Monica by dirt palisades 200 feet high. The top 100 feet of these cliffs were vertical and impassable except for occasional breaks allowing a hazardous descent. Ignoring a nearby concrete stairway, we always chose to climb down. It was slow, laborious, and dangerous. That's why we did it. Climbing down and later back up was, for me, the highlight of the day. Slipping and skidding down the escarpment, grabbing at roots and the odd embedded stone, I felt I was in my natural element. My calling was whispering to me in a soft voice, but I couldn't yet hear what it was saying.

The freedom to come and go as we pleased, one of the special delights of summer, was absolutely precious. We hadn't yet read Mark Twain, but looking back I see it was a Huck Finn period, with the Pacific as our Mississippi.

DANGEROUS EPISODES

Another danger was hitchhiking itself. All sorts of characters picked us up, including sexual predators. We were never bothered in groups of two or three, but when I was alone I had some sinister run-ins with men tempted by a young boy hitchhiking. Their approaches would take the form of a hand on or near my leg, or some suggestion about going somewhere together and "having fun." My reaction was to immediately edge over next to the passenger door and ask to be let out at the next corner. This happened a dozen or so times, and most of the drivers let me out on demand. These easy escapes probably contributed to my self-confidence and underestimation of the real danger. I would walk away angry and annoyed but mostly feeling, as I had with Jim, a mixture of pity and contempt.

Once, however, I had a more serious encounter. On a Saturday, I was heading to the San Gabriel Mountains to explore its hills and canyons. I had gotten a couple of short rides and was standing on a corner in northern Glendale, thumb out, when a man in his twenties stopped and opened the passenger door. I jumped in, closed the door, and thanked him for picking me up. We were driving along a main avenue in La Canada when he made some suggestive remarks, put his hand on my leg, not lightly, but gripping it as if he would hold me there, and turned into a quiet side street. He parked and became aggressive. I knew this time I was really in trouble. Disgusted and full of dread, I also was energized by fear. Realizing that fighting back might get me badly hurt, my mind raced as I tried to stay calm. I found myself thinking with extraordinary clarity. Sensing an opportunity, I said, quietly but with a sense of urgency, "There's someone coming!" Startled, my attacker let go of me and looked up. Seizing my chance, I instantly pushed down the handle, threw open the door, and jumped out, walking quickly away, not looking back.

I guess he just drove off. I never saw him again. I had never heard of child molestation, but I knew these approaches by adults toward kids, and especially this last attack, were wrong, legally as well as in the basic sense of right and wrong. I couldn't be bothered with taking license numbers and turning anyone in. I never felt in actual, serious physical danger, except this once, though I might have been and not realized it. I just wanted to get on with my life and not be bothered.

Although hitchhiking had its dangers, if I was to get where I wanted to go, I had no alternative. I had to take risks. Child molesters were just one of the dangers we daily faced on the streets of L.A. It came with the territory.

HOPPING FREIGHTS

One day, Royal Slagle, Steve Smith, and I, always alert for some new escapade, watched a train lumber slowly out of a freight yard in downtown Los Angeles. Seeing an opportunity, we ran alongside the swaying boxcars, grabbed ladders fastened to their sides, and jumped onto the bottom rungs. After a couple of blocks, we leapt off as the lurching monster picked up speed. Watching the freight disappear into the urban distance, we knew we had discovered a new kind of adventure, one with the intriguing hazard of giant steel wheels rolling close to our legs. And there was more to it. Where were those trains going? What far destinations were they rolling toward, what lands did they go through? We could find out only by riding the rails. The unknown beckoned.

A few days later we were again poised outside the freight yards, impatiently waiting for our magic carpet on rails to pass by. Suddenly, with quickened pulse, we heard the deep hum and throb of the great diesel engines. The pavement quivered under our feet as the train emerged majestically from the yard, slowly picking up speed. There were four diesels pulling an uncountable number of cars. We couldn't wait long. Soon it would be going too fast. We saw our chance – an open door revealed an empty boxcar. Looking right and left and seeing no one who appeared to care, we dashed over and pulled up onto the floor of the boxcar. We were on our way, rolling through the streets of L.A., as free as hobos.

As we approached the northern edge of the big city, the houses and streets and telephone poles streamed by faster and faster. What a lark! My two best friends and I were winging toward some unknown destination. Then we found ourselves leaving the city and entering the mountains. The train climbed slowly over a long pass and then followed a stream down a valley, past groves of sycamores, past intriguing sandstone outcrops, and then out onto a vast desert! Emerging from the mountains onto this scorched plain, I felt cheated. It was monotonous. Where were the trees? It all seemed as dead as the surface of the moon. Little did I know how much I would come to love the special magic of the desert.

After cruising through Palmdale and Lancaster, our iron horse slowed to a trot and then to a walk before stopping on a side track in the town of Mojave to let another train pass in the opposite direction. It was time to return home, so we jumped out of the boxcar and waited hopefully for a ride back to L.A. For several hours we threw rocks at rusty tin cans and practiced balancing on the tracks, until a southbound freight stopped at the siding. Fortunately this train too had an empty boxcar. We crawled in and rode home, arriving unscathed.

Our adventure into the unknown world of train hopping had been a big success. Intoxicated by the heady brew of risk and new vistas, we started hopping freights regularly. Slagle, Smith, and I, never knowing where our train was headed, often found ourselves at strange and exotic locations such as Barstow or San Luis Obispo. Sometimes, after waiting fruitlessly for a train back to Los Angeles, we were forced to hitchhike. In those days, being kids, we could get rides even though there were two or three of us. Rarely looking at maps, we got a practical education in geography by riding freights, reading the highway signs, and thumbing rides.

After our initial few trips, we wearied of sitting on the hard floor of a boxcar as it clicked along mile after mile. So we invented games. One was climbing out of the boxcars by using planks on the sliding

Jumping between trains

doors. To people sitting in autos at railway crossings it must have been startling to see a train thundering past at 60 miles an hour with kids festooning the sides of boxcars. Another game calculated to pass the time was going from one end of the train to the other along the tops of the cars without using our hands. Boxcars presented no problems – you just walked along the steel corrugated walkway and hopped across the short gap to the next car.

Jumping from boxcar to tanker car was more challenging. The rounded top of the tanker was only half as high as the top of the boxcar, and the gap more like 5 feet instead of 3 feet. We managed this several times, and then faced an even tougher challenge: leaping between two tanker cars. This involved an even bigger gap, and we had to jump from the same level. As the train thundered along, swaying from side to side, we would back up, take a running start, and spring into the air across the gap, landing on the distant tanker with a sense of exhilaration, and also a growing and dangerous sense of invulnerability.

Being young and foolish, each of us wanted to be first to do the next daring thing. One day, we were standing atop a boxcar as the train slowed to a crawl. Another freight was pulling out from a siding, passing ours in the opposite direction. The second train seemed close enough to touch, and was creeping along. A seductive idea popped into my brain. Why not jump from one train to another? The gap was only 4 or 5 feet – a simple leap. I saw I could do it – something my friends had not even thought of! Why be afraid?

Why? Because fear can be useful. It can keep you from getting hurt or killed. I almost came to my senses. I started to see my inspiration as madness, but my wild side had taken control. Don't be a chicken, it said. Do it! Jump, you fool!

And so, like a fool, I jumped. The speed of each train was probably only 5 miles an hour, which made a mere 10-mile-an-hour differential. But I had no idea of the forces involved, no way to judge which way to lean or how to land. As soon as my feet touched the metal roof of the boxcar to which I was leaping, my legs were knocked out from under me. I was thrown down on top of the boxcar, rolling over once, twice, and a third time before managing to grab the jagged steel walkway, gashing my hand. That last grab saved me from going off the end of the walkway and falling down between the two boxcars, with consequences too grim to think about. Shaken, I climbed down the ladder and reboarded my original train just as it was slowing to a halt.

My friends said nothing about it, yet I knew they were impressed. I had done something special, something very daring, and this gave me a secret satisfaction. Nevertheless, I never again leapt between trains. It had been a close call, and I knew I was lucky to be alive.

FATHERLESS

When I was ten years old, my mother, hoping to kindle a connection between son and father, sent me to visit my dad. I rode a Greyhound bus to Detroit, where my father met me at the terminal and led me to his apartment – a shabby little room, dark and cheerless. Mom had always spoken highly of Shannon. Whatever his shortcomings, he was a handsome rascal, gallant, and always gentle with her. I was ready to admire him.

Sitting in his living room, I listened intently as Dad talked about all the things he was good at – baseball, boxing, but especially, and much more to my interest, about hunting and being an outdoorsman. He described bear hunts and close calls and was full of outdoor lore. I began to imagine myself walking in my father's footsteps. I had read somewhere that an outdoorsman needed to be a keen observer. Being, by this time, bespectacled, I asked Dad whether one could be good at observing even if one wore glasses. He assured me that good observation wasn't a matter of sharp eyesight but of alertness and concentration. That was reassuring, because I knew by this time that I wanted to be an outdoorsman. It was also reassuring because Dad seemed to be saying that, although I wore glasses, I could be like him.

That's about as close as we got. Mom had shared with me enough of the differences between Jim and Shannon to make the latter sound like a knight in shining armor. I had expected it to be something like Dad and me together, but we awkwardly maintained our distance.

One anecdote paints the picture of my father as I would remember him. Dad and I were strolling the streets of Detroit when he told me of an incident in his life that had occurred a few days earlier. Walking along, he had come to a street corner with a traffic signal. A motorist had carelessly stopped in the crosswalk. As the light changed green for him to walk across, Dad opened the back door of the motorist's car, crawled through, and came out the other side. "I showed him," Dad explained. He had interpreted the motorist's carelessness as an affront and felt obliged to "stand up to him." I guess my father wanted to give me an example of manly behavior, but it seemed to me just foolish, and rather pathetic.

The end result of all this was that I departed feeling Dad was someone I didn't admire and didn't want to spend time with. He may have been equally disappointed in me. He might have thought I was wimpy, overly thoughtful, and not sufficiently resembling the swashbuckling, put-up-your-dukes image he had of his son. I suppose we were both happy to be rid of each other, and I say that now with sadness and regret.

Ah, Dad, why did you leave me? How much have I forgotten, how much have I pushed out of my mind? How have I managed without you all my life? Dad, when did I stop loving you? Can I love you again? What happened back then?

All I got from my two fathers were examples of boorish behavior and self-absorption. I needed something more positive. That came from my mother. In a life of unstable sands, her love was the one unshakable rock. She always let love come first. She didn't talk about it, anymore than she spoke of the Golden Rule, but she lived it. Her love made all the difference in my life.

In addition to that love, she gave me two bits of advice. One was never to treat a woman as she herself had been treated. That I silently vowed. The other, simple and central, was to be good. To Mom, living well required that one be a good person, which to her meant never doing bad things to others. She understood, instinctively, that this was the way to happiness. Resentment was foreign to her nature. She somehow knew that harboring a grudge was like growing a disease in one's soul, and maybe in one's body. She was always generous, sunny, and cheerful, and more often than not she received back in kind what she gave out. From Mom, I got the idea that goodness is superior to evil and that love conquers all.

Love is a mighty virtue, but others, such as honesty, integrity, self-mastery, and perseverance, are important too. Mom had these qualities, but she didn't talk about them. So I would come to discover them on my own, through reading and living and, eventually, through climbing.

BAD TIMES AT JUNIOR HIGH

Although Vine Street Elementary School had seemed to me a soul-searing desert, it was the Garden of Eden compared to Thomas Starr King Junior High, where I enrolled in September 1947. My first day there still hangs, nightmarishly, in my mind. I had to sit in an auditorium with hundreds of other kids, listening to the orientation for new students, learning what we were supposed to do and what not to do. Vine Street Elementary was, by comparison, homey, gentle, and personalized. This was a big institution, with teachers dedicated to helping children move toward adulthood. Our principal, Dr. Struthers, was a short, stout lady who affected a monocle and, like Wyatt Earp, always wore black. Her severe bearing and eyeglass gave her the look of a righteous avenger. As punishment for being bad, we were actually put on a "hot seat" and given light electric shocks. Also, when she felt it was deserved, she whacked us with a bamboo rod. After once feeling its sting, you carefully avoided behavior that called it into play.

In class, I continued to flounder. I couldn't get things right. I didn't understand the lessons. At times I would work diligently, determined to improve my grades, but it was no use. I kept my place at the bottom of the class. Since hard work didn't help, I lost the motivation to try.

Of course I didn't then realize what hard work meant. I somehow had bought into the comically flawed notion that life is not supposed to be hard. I suppose I got this idea by observing the apparently effortless success of my peers, at studies, sports, and social activities. I didn't realize that much of the excellence I saw around me was less due to brains and physical coordination and social aptitude than to resiliency and toughness and spunk. I had some growing up to do.

Wood shop, at least, provided a brief moment of glory. I had taken on a project of making for my mother a wooden, three-shelved corner piece to hold photos and art objects. I worked at it long and carefully and was at last pleased with the result. I was even more pleased when the instructor complimented me in front of the class. I was just starting to glow with self-satisfaction when a fellow student piped up, "It took him an awful long time, didn't it?" That was a slap in the face, but I could have weathered that sneering comment had not the instructor immediately agreed, "Yes, you're right. If you all took that long we wouldn't get much done around here." My swelling pride was instantly flattened by the steamroller of my instructor's dismissal.

To hell with it then. Why had I let myself hope? I knew I was a loser. So much for compliments, so much for wood shop, so much for painstaking attention to getting it right. Our instructor might have said, "Yes, it took him a bit long, but that's OK. What counts is doing it right. What counts is a finished product of quality!" That might have made a difference in my life. It certainly would have made a difference in wood shop. Economics demands speed and efficiency, but the human soul feeds upon excellence, beauty, and the pursuit of perfection.

At a deeper level I still couldn't quite believe I was truly a loser. Somewhere in my reading I had come across a story of eminent men who had been poor students. They had been weak at studies simply because they were too smart for school. They were geniuses. Churchill and Einstein were among those mentioned. Ah, here was a life pre-server thrown to this drowning lad! Maybe I was a poor student because I was so smart! With rising hope, I went to look into this.

In those days school psychologists routinely gave students intel-ligence tests. The records of such tests were kept in the school office and available upon demand. I went to the office and requested the results of my IQ tests. The school psychologist had retested me sev-eral times in an unsuccessful attempt to determine why I got such terrible grades. He told me, "Royal, I just can't figure you out. I can understand all the other kids who come in here, but you're a mystery." I took a secret pride in being indecipherable. In that, at least, there always lurked the chance of some hidden brilliance.

A lady behind the counter handed me the papers. There were three sets of numbers from three separate tests. They varied a little, but the message was unmistakable: I was not stupid. Nor was I smart. I was average. My heart sank. The dry wind of a battery of tests with-ered my hopes of being a closet genius. It is less true today, but back then IQ tests were thought to be accurate predictors of how well one would do in the great game of life. For me, it seemed the game was up. I was doomed to a life of mediocrity. I might have thanked God for at least not making me a dolt, but I was not in a grateful mood.

KING OF THE MOUNTAIN

Although I was just average at traditional athletics, I did well at a couple of games of my own invention, both schoolyard forms of King of the Mountain. In one, two "gladiators" stood atop a bench 1 foot wide and 8 feet long and tried to knock each other off. The rule that one hand be kept behind one's back made it more a game of quickness and balance than of strength. At times we would have a dozen boys in line at the end of the bench waiting to take on the winner.

The other game, a complex variation of the bench contest, took place at the east end of the schoolyard, on a 50-foot-long section of ground that sloped up to about 8 feet above the yard. The first 4 feet were vertical, held in place by a wall of wooden planks. Above the wood, the ground sloped up at 45 degrees to a wire fence marking the edge of the school property. The goal of this free-for-all was to push your opponent off the slope before he did the same to you. Once off, the player was "dead" until everyone was down, leaving only one boy as King of the Mountain. Then we would start over.

To begin, we would all get up on the embankment and, when someone gave the signal, start pushing, throwing kids off left and right. Being smaller than average, I was quick, agile, and slippery, inclined to use my foe's weight and size against him. I had so much fun at this game that it was almost worthwhile coming to school. We played every morning before classes began. Soon, more and more students joined in. We started arriving an hour before classes to play King of the Mountain. At times there were nearly two dozen kids throwing each other off the mountain.

I had a feeling Dr. Struthers wouldn't approve, but we got away with this game for months, probably because we played in the morning before school started. Finally a boy got hurt, and King of the Mountain was banned. Though disappointed to see my favorite pastime go, at least I had found something for which I had a talent. It was just a crumb, but one crumb here and another there – that's nourishment!

CHAPTER IV

Turning Point

The holdup

FLIRTING WITH THE DEVIL

My early transgressions were no more sinister than young Frodo Baggins filching mushrooms from Farmer Maggot's field. At age 12, however, I crossed the divide between venturesome boy and premeditating criminal. It began with an invitation, placed in our mailbox, to a boys' camp. My happiest days had been at the YMCA camp, so anything with the word "camp" was a flame to this young moth. The trouble was, unlike the YMCA camp, which had been free, this one cost $50. Where could we get $50? We didn't have any money, certainly not that much. Nevertheless I begged Mom to let me go. I couldn't see past my own desires. Camp meant freedom, joy, and new friends. I could run and shout and be myself. Camp was escape from the humdrum streets of Los Angeles.

I tried to wear Mom down by again and again pleading my case, but she was resolute: "I'm sorry, Royal. I know how much it means to you, but we can't afford it, and you *know* that. So forget it and do your homework!"

Stung by this painful evidence of life's unfairness, I vented my complaints to an uncaring Master of the Universe: My friends were going, but we couldn't afford it. Other kids got to go; why shouldn't I? I wanted to go even more than they did. Why should I be denied? God didn't seem to give a hang for my predicament, so I said the hell with him and became the devil's disciple. I had to go, and I wasn't going to take no for an answer. I decided to become a desperado.

I owned a toy pistol that I liked to brandish in our mock shootouts. It was black, and I thought it would look real enough to a startled victim, especially at night. I decided to test this theory. One evening after dark I slipped the pretend pistol into my pocket, walked a few blocks west to a more upscale neighborhood, and turned north on Las Palmas Avenue.

And there he was, about 50 feet away, a man wearing a coat and tie walking toward me. Suddenly my mind filled with doubt: This is crazy! I can't do this! I'll just walk by him, I thought. Yes, that was the thing to do. As I shuffled along the sidewalk I felt immensely relieved I had decided to not go through with this mad scheme. But then something within me began to taunt: "You chicken, you coward. You sissy! Do it!"

I couldn't stand being called names, so, when I was 6 feet from the man, who towered above me, I pulled out my pistol, pointed it up at him, and said, "Stick 'em up!" He stopped, but he didn't stick 'em up. He looked at me in a curious, kindly way, and said, "What do you want?" I replied, as sternly as I could manage, "Your money!"

"Certainly," he said, with a smile that confused me. What was he grinning about? He reached into his back pocket and pulled out his wallet. Oh boy, I thought. This is easy! Then he pulled a single dollar from his billfold and offered it to me.

My self-confidence changed instantly to deep chagrin. My worst fears were coming true. A dollar, I thought. What am I going to do with a dollar? Would I have to do 50 holdups to get enough money to go to camp? What was this guy doing? Trying to make a fool of me? Not that I wasn't doing a good job of that myself. I realized he was toying with me. He must have seen the gun for what it was – a toy. I lacked the gumption to say, "No monkey business! I want all of your money, or else!" Acutely aware of my idiocy, I pocketed my pistol and slunk past him, into the night.

He has stayed with me all these years. He must have been a good man. He could have crushed me with one blow, or grabbed me by the collar and dragged me off to the police station. Pulling a stunt like that, only a few blocks from my own house, was proof that I was no master criminal. How does one explain such reckless folly? Perhaps I was, once again, searching for lines that must not be crossed.

That single botched attempt at getting money the easy way convinced me that I was not cut out for a career in armed robbery. So I missed camp that summer. I trod the straight and narrow for the rest of the year, then strayed again, this time into burglary. My accomplices were my train-hopping and bodysurfing chums, Steve Smith and Royal Slagle.

We weren't run-of-the-mill burglars. We might not have realized it, but money was a secondary goal. We liked money and had plenty of uses for it, but our burglaries were more about adventure. We didn't break into homes when people were away, or into businesses that were closed. We didn't steal valuable objects to fence. That was too complicated and sophisticated for us. We only broke into houses when people were at home.

Our method was to slip into backyards and peer through windows, looking for purses. Often they were sitting right next to a bedroom window that in southern California commonly was left open, even in the middle of winter. With only a screen separating us from the purse, we pierced the metal mesh with a nail and dislodged the locking hook. Carefully opening the screen, we emptied the purse of any money, put it back, and quietly closed the screen. The purse's owner was probably rarely aware that outsiders had had a hand in her finances. We might have gotten a few husbands in trouble! On a few occasions we caught sight of a purse across the room and one of us, usually me, actually climbed into the room while members of the family were in the next room talking and moving about. This was really risky, but part of the fun was seeing how much we could get away with, like a bullfighter coming close to the horns without being gored.

It never occurred to me what the Hardy Boys might have thought of this. In any case, we still saw ourselves as the good guys. We took only money. It was a point of honor never to cause serious trouble to our victims. We got a wallet once and, hearing someone coming, ran off with it. The next night, we walked past the home and tossed the wallet on the front porch so the owner would have his driver's license and other personal papers. We weren't hardened criminals, just kids having fun and making off with a little extra money people didn't need anyway. Or so we told ourselves.

These petty burglaries became irresistible. We couldn't stop. Every successful job convinced us we were too smart to end up in jail. Had we been thinking clearly, we would have concluded that we'd better give this up before we got caught, but there was no corrective inner voice of reason. It would take an outside voice, which soon arrived.

One night early in December 1947, we three screen-piercers were emerging from the backyard of a house when a police car rounded the corner and braked to a halt. Before the cops could get out of their car, we were racing pell-mell in different directions, confident in our running and scrambling ability. I headed for a fence to jump over into another backyard. I was nearly over and safe, thinking no policeman was even close, when one of them shouted, "You'd better give up. We've got your buddies." His confident tone convinced me he was telling the truth. I dropped from the fence and walked slowly toward the patrol car, shoulders drooping, overcome with shame.

The sad memory of the three of us sitting in the back of the police car, giving our personal information, still haunts me. All I could think was, This is going to be terrible. Poor Mom. This is a nightmare. Alas, I wasn't dreaming. We had been really stupid, and we were going to have to pay the price.

I couldn't believe they were actually taking us to jail. We were just kids. We weren't really bad. It was our first offense. Surely they would let us go with just a warning. Nope. To the jailhouse we went. The fingerprinting. The interrogation: "Where did you get the idea of doing this?" It was a question they kept asking, assuming we couldn't have thought up the scheme ourselves and suspecting some adult had put us up to it.

We were, indeed, just kids, so they took us to juvenile hall, where we spent the night locked in cells – jailbirds! The three of us got separated. It was a big place. The next morning, guards herded a big group of us to breakfast in an enormous dining room, and then out into the barren yard for jumping jacks and push-ups. There I was, with all the other troublemakers, surrounded by concrete and steel. It wasn't a bad dream. It was real. I was a criminal.

They didn't mistreat us physically; they had subtler ways of taking away our dignity. The toilets were a degrading experience. As with eating and exercising, they took us in large groups. The toilets were close together in a long row, without partitions. We stood in a line, awaiting our turn. Deeply embarrassed, I avoided looking at those using the toilets. When it was my turn, I avoided the eyes of those waiting. It seemed disgraceful to take away your privacy. It robbed you of your self-respect as a human being. I longed with an aching heart for the freedom to walk down a street, to turn left or right or cross over whenever I pleased. Freedom had never appeared so precious. I had to get out of jail, and when I did I would forsake the road that had led me there.

After several days of incarceration, we were released to the custody of our parents. Two weeks later it was time for the hearing. Mom took me to the courthouse and pleaded before the judge for my freedom. She said I was a good boy, I had a good heart, and she knew I would never do anything bad again. She would see to it. She believed in me, and she would keep me out of trouble. Thank God, the judge was convinced. He let me go. I owe Mom a lot for that. Her eloquence, and her belief in me, and most of all her love, saved me. Steve Smith was also released, though he and I rarely saw each other again. Royal Slagle's parents, tired of a troublesome son, told the magistrate, "There's nothing we can do with him." So back to jail Slagle went. Many years later I heard he was in prison, in Susanville, California.

GOING STRAIGHT

My freedom restored, I was determined to walk the straight and narrow. I would be like one of the Hardy Boys, the opposite of a crook.

Looking for a way to make a commitment to that ideal, I joined the Boy Scouts, the best decision of my young life. In January 1948, Mom and I looked up "Boy Scouts" in the telephone book and called the Los Angeles Council. I was assigned to a unit in my area, Troop 127. This organization had the special distinction of being known as the Rainbow Troop

It also had the distinction of an unusual sponsor: the Los Angeles Police Department. In an ironic twist, fate was giving me the opportunity to mend relations with the men in blue. Our Scoutmaster, Phil Bailey, a police officer, was a tall, cheerful man, a model of strength and courage seasoned with courtesy and gentleness. He was just what I needed for a surrogate dad – a combination of Jimmy Stewart and John Wayne.

THE RAINBOW TROOP

When I joined the Rainbow Troop early in 1948, Phil Bailey's goal was to build not just another troop, but "a troop that kids would be proud of." He was already leading Troop 127 in new and original directions. The troop uniform, unique in southern California, required short-sleeved shirts and shorts with knee-length socks, following the design of Scouting's founder, Lord Baden-Powell. There were four patrols, each consisting of eight to ten boys. Each patrol was distinguished by a different name and color. The kids chose the names: Red Ravens, Blue Beavers, Golden Eagles, and Purple Panthers. I became a Purple Panther and was given a purple neckerchief. Our patrol leader was Rod Halphide.

I thought all these distinctions that set us apart from other troops were pretty cool. They helped build a sense of pride in our troop and in Scouting as well. After all, why shouldn't each troop be known for something special? Why shouldn't each troop be unique? In addition, these adventurous differences introduced a playful element. They helped make Scouting what it should be – fun.

A FULL HOUSE

In July of 1948, my mother and sister and I left Seward Street in yet another move. Times were tough, and Mom struggled to make ends meet. A solution arose in the form of generous relatives, my uncle Bill Chandler (Jim's brother) and his wife, Velma. They lived with their two daughters, Una and Linda, in a four-bedroom house on Commonwealth Avenue in northeastern Hollywood. They took us in for a lot less money than it cost to live at Seward Street. At the same time, they also took in other relatives. These were Jim's sister, Audrey, her husband, Harold Metcalf, their two sons, Tom and Homer, and their two daughters, Ann and Jan. There were 13 of us – quite a household. All of us ate together, and everyone got along, pulling together in a

Troop 127 (The Rainbow Troop) Patch

time of need. The Metcalfs and we owe a lot to Bill and Velma, and to their vision that we could all live together happily and comfortably.

My sister, Helen (we knew her as "Penny"), was at this time seven years old. She was a sweet child, smiling and friendly, though cursed with a selfish ogre of a brother who had to have his way. I insisted on listening to my type of music and to my favorite radio programs. Mom usually let me win because I would argue louder and more forcefully, and because if I didn't get my way I would cause more trouble pouting and whining than my sister would. Penny and I, even though we didn't share many interests, have always been close and loving half-siblings, especially if I got my way.

Homer and I were the same age. He joined the Rainbow Troop and became a fellow Purple Panther. When we weren't Scouting, we each earned money hawking newspapers, the *Herald Express* and the *Daily News*, on busy intersections. My assigned corner was Santa Monica Boulevard and Vermont Avenue. I spent many an afternoon there waving papers, shouting out "Heraaald-a-News!" and dodging automobiles.

Homer and I played together, but we were never close. Beneath the surface ran a constant undercurrent of competition. I always wanted to beat Homer at whatever we were playing but rarely did. When we played chess, Homer usually won. When we wrestled, which was something I thought myself pretty good at, Homer usually won, though he was smaller than me. He did well in school and got good grades, unlike me. But at least in climbing, what little climbing we did together, I could hold my own. Homer lived up to the intellectual promise of his youth, later becoming a professor of philosophy at Chico State University in northern California.

We lived within walking distance of Griffith Park, an extensive preserve occupying much of the chaparral-covered Hollywood Hills that separated Tinsel Town from the San Fernando Valley. We went there to hike but usually ended up off the trail, crawling on our hands and knees beneath the manzanita and buckthorn, always careful to avoid the widespread poison oak. Bee Rock, a 300-foot outcrop on the east side of the park, attracted us as a diversion from hiking or clawing through the brush. Homer and I often scrambled around on its treacherous conglomerate. Occasionally Homer's sisters, Ann and Jan, joined us, and Penny as well. The girls didn't like climbing on Bee Rock, especially Penny, who got dizzy on the gentle apron below the steep part. Fifty years later, she and her two cousins could vividly describe those outings.

THE SCOUTING LIFE

Many boys enter Scouting with their characters already formed by family, church, sports organizations, and other institutions. For those like me, whose existence was not held together by a set of good habits, one of the benefits of the Scouting life was to instill a sense of discipline and order. In Troop 127, this encouragement to master oneself took the form of semi-military drills and spit and polish. We learned Right march! Left march! About face! Parade rest! We were expected to arrive at meetings on time, with clean fingernails and shined shoes. It wasn't excessive, but it kept us aware of the difference between sloppiness and crispness in appearance, thinking, and action.

We studied the *Boy Scout Handbook* and learned the Scout Oath and the famous Scout Motto: "Be prepared." The Scout Slogan was

"Do a good turn daily." Wanting to be a good Scout, I looked for every chance to do a good turn. I still remember vividly my first one: I helped an elderly lady across the street and carried her groceries to her home. She wanted to give me 50 cents, which in those days was a lot of money, but I politely refused, knowing that taking money would cancel the goodness of my deed. As time passed, I noticed that my fellow Scouts didn't talk about good deeds. I guessed we were supposed to keep our good acts to ourselves. Aware, however, of the lack of emphasis in our troop on good deeds, my initial zealotry faded. But I have never forgotten the lesson learned there – that we have a duty to do good to others.

Scouting was a lifesaver that kept me from drowning in a sea of anarchy and aimlessness. The Scouts got me out of the streets of L.A. and up into the mountains, into the out-of-doors. We stayed at Boy Scout camps in the Los Angeles area, including Pepperdine, from which I scribbled a card to my mother:

13 August 1948 – Dear Mother, our Hikemaster just spilt some Loomburger cheese on the floor. it made me sick. I will be home fridy.

In one case, we bicycled to camp. Our leaders gave us maps and expected us to find our way, which we did, in small groups. Thus the Rainbow Troop stayed true to Scouting's mission of building self-reliance. Gershon Weltman, one of the Scouts in my patrol, later would produce an extremely well-written guide to bicycling in Los Angeles.

We also took hiking and backpacking trips lasting up to seven days in the nearby mountains. In the evening around a fire we sang rousing songs, for me one of the highlights of camping. On and on,

into the night, we chorused with lyrics from "The Blue-Tail Fly" and
"Green Grow the Rushes Ho!" We also belted out "99 Bottles of Beer
on the Wall" and "Little Brown Jug," songs that might be disapproved
of today. Somehow I happened upon the Intercollegiate Outing Club
Association (IOCA) songbook, a treasure trove of songs for group
singing. Some of the numbers were brilliantly nonsensical, such as
the "Vassar Hygiene Song," which included these lyrics:

Oh we never used to bathe
till we heard the Doctor rave
In the lectures that she gave
how to behave;
Now we take our daily bath
even though we miss our math.
How in the world do you know that?
She told us so.

I had a soft spot for "The Horses Run Around":

The horses run around,
their feet are on the ground,
Oh, who will wind the clock
while I'm away, away,
Go get the axe, there's
a hair on baby's chest;
Oh, a boy's best friend is
his mother, his mother.

From IOCA Songbook

I memorized many of those songs, including all 19 stanzas of "Abdullah Bulbul Amir," the son of the prophet, who wages an epic battle with the Czarist warrior Ivan Skavinsky Skivar:

> They parried and thrust,
> they sidestepped and cussed,
> Of blood they spilled a great part;
> The philologist blokes,
> who seldom crack jokes,
> Say that hash was first made on that spot.

OUTDOOR EXPERT

Camping, hiking, songfests around the campfire, and simply being outdoors all helped me leave behind, in mind and spirit, the urban world of Los Angeles. The outdoors suited me and I took to it as a fish to water. Our senior patrol leader, Leon Robb, ever alert to potential in the younger boys around him, asked me to plan our camping trips. The duties included planning menus, getting supplies, and even choosing a camping location. My qualifications were rooted in my habit of hitchhiking into the San Gabriel Mountains north of Los Angeles to wander ridges and canyons. Responding to Leon's direction, I planned a successful outing to a public camp no one in the troop had ever visited, along Arroyo Seco Creek, west of Mount Wilson in the Angeles National Forest. The success of this trip fueled my desire to pour more of my energies into outdoor action. I owe a lot to Leon for giving me these chances to use what talents I had.

Sierra Patrol Award Ceremony
(Royal in Scout uniform, Scoutmaster Bailey in police uniform)

Flush with my new field responsibilities, I unconsciously slipped into the role of "outdoor expert." I didn't think about it, and I didn't try for the distinction. It simply came naturally. In May 1949 I joined Leon Robb and two other boys from our troop, along with Mr. Bailey, on a trip to Yosemite Valley. Our goal was to check out camping sites and hiking paths. This was my introduction to the wonderland of walls and waterfalls that would eventually mold my character and guide my destiny. I little imagined, in that first vision of Yosemite's great rocks, how many nights I would lie awake high on a ledge, shivering in the early morning hours, waiting for the dawn.

THE SIERRA PATROL

One day Mr. Bailey pulled me aside and informed me I had been selected as our troop's Top Outdoor Scout and would therefore be going on a special outing to the Sierra Nevada. I was astonished. I knew there were many boys in our troop who were much better Scouts than I was. They had more merit badges. They were unit leaders. They were better at drill and so forth. I thought the things I did in the outdoor arena were nothing compared to their achievements. I had earned a few merit badges, so I was well aware of how much hard work each one required. But my outdoor skills just came naturally, and seemed easier, so I discounted them.

Looking back, however, I realize I was the Scout in our troop who, more than any other, would get into the mountains whenever I could, often alone, to hike and explore. I was the Scout who found hidden campsites and later planned and organized troop outings to these choice spots. Perhaps I was a reasonable choice for this honor. Still, it somehow didn't seem right. I merely did what I loved doing. I didn't know then what I know now, that achievement and having fun are natural partners.

My reward for being Top Outdoor Scout was a ten-day back-packing trip into the High Sierra. This wilderness excursion, known as the Sierra Patrol, was a gift of radio station KFI, where one could tune in once a week to the renowned "Scoutmaster of the Air," Clem Glass. Glass had led these trips in 1946 and 1947 with the help of a young man just out of the Air Force named Al Wilkes. Al was another Scoutmaster, like Phil Bailey, who would become a personal hero to me and strongly influence the direction my life would take.

Mr. Bailey took me to the awards ceremony and stood there, erect and smiling, in his police uniform as I, beaming with pride, received the award. It was the happiest moment of my life, and a very long way from juvenile hall. I had found a better path. And now I was going to the High Sierra!

On a Friday morning at the end of June 1949, the Top Outdoor Scouts from various L.A. troops gathered at the KFI parking lot in downtown Los Angeles, ready for the journey north.

Our instructions had been to bring certain necessities but to keep our packs as light as possible. We would be supported by pack animals carrying the food, cooking equipment, tents, and so on, but we were to tote our personal gear. I didn't own a sleeping bag, but I'd learned from my Boy Scout handbook how to fold two blankets to make a bed roll. So I brought along a couple of wool army-surplus blankets that I had used on camping trips. They had always kept me warm enough in the southern California mountains, but I was to learn that the Sierra Nevada was not only higher but also colder. I should have taken another blanket or two, but I was terrified at the prospect of not being able to keep up with the other Top Outdoor Scouts.

I arrived at the meeting place early in the morning to find two dozen boys milling about. Leaders checked our gear and weighed our packs. I had succeeded in my efforts to go light – my pack weighed only 17 pounds, the lightest of them all. The smallest boy in the group had the heaviest pack – 35 pounds.

At noon we piled into a flatbed truck with side panels and headed off, following the Angeles Forest Highway over the San Gabriel Mountains to Palmdale. As we sped north across the Mojave Desert, I fondly remembered those train-hopping adventures with Smith and Slagle. This time I would be going much farther.

We drove through the towns of Lancaster and Mojave, and then through country I hadn't seen before. As the hours passed, the other Scouts relaxed in the bed of the truck. I stayed at the rail, hair and bandanna flying in the wind, taking it all in.

We were on Highway 395 now, in a new landscape known as the Owens Valley. Tall mountain ranges rose on each side, the Sierra Nevada to the west and the Inyos to the east. From books and maps I had learned that soon we would see the highest mountain in the United States at that time, Mount Whitney. From my perch I watched as the Sierra peaks grew taller and more rugged with each passing mile.

As we passed through the town of Lone Pine I searched the high peaks to the west for Whitney. A spectacular group of bold ridges and sculpted faces rose 10,000 feet above the valley. I wasn't sure which of the pointed summits was Whitney, but it didn't matter – they were all high, distant, and beckoning.

As we continued north up 395, I kept watching as new mountains came into view. We would soon be in that high wonderland-hiking, wrangling pack animals, being real outdoorsmen! In late afternoon, dusty and parched, but full of enthusiasm, we finally reached what was to be our springboard into the High Sierra, the little town of Independence. We camped there in a city park.

The next morning I was up at dawn watching the rising sun bathe the white granite of the Sierra in golden light. Though I hadn't yet read John Muir, I would remember this first dawn view of these mountains when I learned of his famous nickname for the Sierra Nevada: not the snowy range (its translation from the Spanish), but the Range of Light.

After a hearty breakfast of ham, eggs, and pancakes, and more ham, and more eggs, and more pancakes, we drove from Independence up a narrow, high-angle dirt road loaded with switchbacks and hairpin turns to the 9,200-foot trailhead at Onion Valley. The loaded burros greeted us with sleepy eyes. They knew all too well what to expect in the coming days. We were soon on our way, trudging steeply upward. Above us, great walls of white granite stood guard like towering sentinels, welcoming us to their magical land – or warning us, depending on your point of view.

We progressed slowly toward the distant pass, step by step, as Independence Creek, with its early summer flow, thundered alongside the trail. Light winds coursed through the trees, providing a welcome coolness on the hot and dusty trail. The pine needles barely moved in the breeze, but the leaves of the quaking aspens shimmered with each gust.

It was going well – not too hard, and I was holding my own. Yet I kept noticing, as I looked down the switchbacks, that the little fellow with the big pack, Ben, was lagging behind. In fact, as we got higher, he was going slower and slower. I gave a big inward sigh as I realized what I had to do – a good deed! I stepped off the trail and waited until Ben got to me and then offered to trade packs: "Hi! Say, I'm feeling good and my pack is pretty light. Wanna change for awhile?" To my hidden disappointment, he gratefully accepted. Now carrying a pack half the weight he had been lugging, Ben moved briskly and he easily kept up with the others. I followed behind, now toting not the lightest pack but the heaviest. Although I had said "for awhile," I ended up shouldering Ben's pack for the rest of the trip. It was tough, but it was good for me. It made me stronger.

Up there the air was thin and pure, and I was panting as we topped Kearsarge Pass at 11,823 feet. After resting, we descended 1,200 feet to our first campsite at Bullfrog Lake. We were now in the heart of the High Sierra, with rock peaks jutting on every side into a cloudless sky. I was in paradise. We set up camp and then enjoyed serving after serving of a delicious stew. When we could eat no more, we sang songs around the campfire until deep into the night. Then, exhausted after a very long and very full day, we hit the sack. I fell instantly into a deep sleep but sometime in the early morning hours I woke up shivering. The temperature had taken a nosedive. Even with all my clothes on inside the two blankets I was too cold to sleep. The camp was utterly still but the campfire was still glowing, just a few

Glen Pass　　　　　　　　　　　　　　　　　　*Photo: Al Wilkes*

yards away. I rolled over a few times and curled up next to the dying embers. The slowly fading warmth enabled me to sleep until the welcome rays of the morning sun peeked over the ridges. It became a nightly habit to snuggle next to the fire to keep warm.

The next day, we hiked over Glen Pass toward our base camp at Rae Lakes. Glen Pass, at 11,987 feet, is a low point on a ridge amid the surrounding mountains, yet it is higher than the tallest peaks in southern California. There, Mounts San Gorgonio, San Jacinto, and Baldy are monarchs, but they can only hint at the glory of the High Sierra. From the pass, we were treated to views of mountain cirques surrounded by sharp peaks. To the north, south, and east, continuous palisades offered endless opportunities for exploration and adventure. To the west, ridges and canyons descended gently into the soft haze of the hot Central Valley. Up on the pass, the air was cool and refreshing.

Then we were hiking down, behind the pack animals. Typical of early July at this elevation, snow still covered parts of the trail. Down, down we went, to a sparkling, pine-bordered lake that would be our camp for several days. Other small lakes nestled nearby, courtesy of the ancient scooping glaciers. The lakes were connected to each other by an interlacing system of small meadows and streams, with granite slabs rising above them toward sky-piercing peaks.

The next morning we were treated to a stupendous breakfast of stacks of pancakes overflowing with butter and syrup, and all the bacon we could eat, which was plenty. It briefly soothed our hunger, but it seemed we were always famished and always eating. After breakfast, while the other boys fished or played games in camp, I wandered up grass slopes and climbed polished granite slabs to discover a group of

Fin Dome   *Photo: Ed Cooper*

pools and small lakes. No breath of morning air rippled their surfaces. Bordered with bright green grass and white granite boulders, they were perfectly transparent, touchingly beautiful.

This was life at its best: coming and going as I pleased, wandering off alone, hiking and climbing about, seeing new beauties and vistas. I fell in love with this Sierran world of granite and light, of lakes and streams, meadows and forests, deer and marmots. Most of all, the great white slabs and towering peaks called to my heart. I didn't yet know how to answer, but I was soon to learn.

FIN DOME

That evening, between campfire songs, one of our leaders, Mr. Walder, offered us the chance to climb a nearby mountain called Fin Dome. It's not really a mountain, and it's not really a dome, but this peak, shaped like a shark's fin, rises 1,200 feet above dozens of crystal-clear lakes. Standing alone above the surrounding landscape, Fin Dome had caught my eye the previous day when we were descending from Glen Pass. I had instinctively wanted to reach its summit, but it seemed too high, too remote, too tough. So I put it from my mind. Now it had come back into focus.

Mr. Walder asked for volunteers, and my arm shot up instantly. Three other arms rose high, and our party was set – four boys and two adult leaders, Mr. Walder and Mr. Thompson. The other boys were Don, tall and lean, with a long, serious face; Bruce, a cheerful and excitable kid about my age and size; and, of all people, little Ben, the boy whose pack I had been carrying. Ben seemed kind of soft and round, but he was game. He wanted to climb a mountain, so I thought he must be OK.

The next morning, we mountaineers silently arose in the darkness while our fellow campers continued to saw logs. It was my first "alpine start." The idea is to get up and off the peaks before thunderclouds build or the sun loosens rocks embedded in ice. Even if these dangers aren't present, an early start is wise, because if something goes wrong, as often happens, you have more daylight to sort out the difficulties.

Skipping breakfast, we shouldered our packs and ropes and were quickly off. Flashlights showed the way as we followed the path toward our peak. After an hour, we left the trail to hike cross-country, just as light began to fill the sky over the toothed ridges to the east. We switched off our flashlights and kept going. As we came over a rise, sunlight touched the highest peaks and, suddenly, there it was: Fin Dome, a mighty tower rising into the sky. To us, it was as glorious as the Matterhorn.

It made my heart pound just to see it. This was something quite new, no mere hike or treasure hunt. Well, yes, it *was* a treasure hunt, for real treasure: a tiny summit, high in the sky. Soon this treasure would be ours!

Fin Dome is composed of steep slabs of smooth granite. We were going to climb its west face, where the slabs were broken by cracks and ledges. This was the most accessible side, but it wasn't going to be easy. Our leaders had chosen a steeper section, to give us experience in roped climbing.

Before starting, we reviewed climbing signals. "Belay on!" meant "I am protecting you with the rope!" "Climbing!" was said by the person ready to go, but he didn't move until the belayer gave permission by saying "Climb!" We were told to shout "Slack!" when we wanted less tightness in the rope, and "Up rope!" when we wanted the line taken in. It is important to be clear about a signal, because if you are around a corner or it is windy and you shout "Take in slack!" your belayer might only hear "Slack!" and give you more rope, the opposite of what you want.

We had brought two 100-foot nylon ropes, so we tied in at 50-foot intervals, three to a rope. The leader used a bowline knot, as did the last climber, while Ben and I, who were in the middle of our respective ropes, used an overhand loop, stepping into it and then pulling it up and making it tight around our waists. After checking our knots, Mr. Walder led off. I was second on his rope and Don brought up the rear. Mr. Thompson led the other rope, with Ben next. Bruce brought up the rear, joking and grinning as usual. The leader of each rope would climb about 40 feet, reach a ledge, and set up a belay. Then he would bring first one and then the other Scout up to his stance before continuing.

When the command "Climb!" came from above, I eagerly set off, pulling here, pushing there, leaning and reaching for holds. Blessed with a degree of agility, I clambered like a monkey up the short rock steps formed by successive blocks of granite. Stretching to reach the edge of a shelf, I would pull up onto it, and then push down with arms straight, raising a foot and standing up, ready for the next problem. The movements came naturally, as if climbing was in my blood.

I was at ease with the steepness and the exposure. Danger was always there, of course, waiting to snag the unwary. This was, after all, no amusement park. We boys were doing serious, grown-up stuff.

At 11 a.m. we six stood on top, shaking hands. It was my initiation into this time-honored ritual of celebrating success on top of a mountain. It was a big moment. As I grasped the hands of my companions, one by one, I felt I was being welcomed into a special club: the brotherhood of the rope. Our guides had climbed with packs containing the lunches and water, except for a big metal army-surplus canteen Don insisted on carrying around his shoulder all the way up. Having missed breakfast we turned eagerly to lunch, breaking out peanut butter sandwiches, apples, and cookies, which we washed down with what was left of our water.

As we sat on the summit, wolfing the food down, we surveyed our domain like kings – the lakes, the rolling granite, the meadows and forests, all spread out beneath us. Beautifully sculpted spires rose on all sides. This was the wonderland of the High Sierra and we were in the heart of it. We weren't just visitors or mere sightseers. We had struggled and climbed a mountain. We had earned the right to be part of all this.

With the sun directly overhead and no cloud in sight, we began the descent of the regular route, climbing unroped down gullies and rock steps, not far from the line we had ascended. Halfway down we rested on a ledge. Don forgot his canteen there. He remembered it at the base of the peak, but we all agreed it wasn't worth climbing back up for it.

I was lucky to survive that descent. Still excited by our triumph, and unrestrained by the rope, I dashed down, jumping from ledge to ledge and block to block, fearlessly flinging myself downward. I saw the care and caution my mates were displaying, but I felt superior to all that. Intoxicated with my newfound ability, I acted the fool and very nearly paid the ultimate price. In my exuberance, I jumped too hard and too far and careened out of control, stopping just in time on my tiptoes right at the sharp lip of a ledge of granite, my momentum very nearly carrying me off the edge and down a hundred feet. Backing away from the void, I glanced back at my companions, happy to realize none of them had seen how close I had come to death. Showing off had nearly gotten me killed, so from then on I descended cautiously, one step at a time, the rest of the way to the bottom of the peak. From there we made our way first cross-country and then by trail back to camp. Having reached a superb summit, we returned filled with joy and eager for more.

I had been taught a priceless lesson. I had learned there was a power within me that I hadn't dreamt existed, a power to climb. I had looked through a magic window and found something of great depth and wonder, something I was made for. Fin Dome was a turning point.

CHAPTER V

Early Climbs

A REAL CLIMB, ON MY OWN

After my Fin Dome experience in July 1949, I returned to Los Angeles, hungry for opportunities to climb. They weren't plentiful. Mountaineering was not part of the repertoire of the Rainbow Troop. So I climbed buildings, fences, and trees, anything that would get me above the ground and help me feel like a *climber*. Of course, there was some danger in this clambering around without a rope, but I was full of self-confidence. I had no idea I was an accident waiting to happen.

Before going to the High Sierra I had often hitchhiked into the San Gabriels to hike trails and wander peaks. I resumed this habit, but now I never missed the chance to scramble up the odd outcrop or rocky slope. I wanted to sharpen my climbing skills in every way possible. Remembering the lessons learned on Fin Dome, I soon turned to roped climbing, revisiting Bee Rock occasionally, as well as the San Gabriels.

I couldn't afford a nylon rope like those we used on Fin Dome. Such ropes, greatly superior to natural fibers, were far too expensive for my meager allowance. Reasoning that any rope was better than none, I appropriated lengths of Manila hemp that had been discarded by trucking companies as worthless. At army-surplus stores I purchased climbing gear made for the mountain troops in World War II: soft iron pitons for 25 cents each, heavy steel snap links called carabiners for 75 cents, and a piton hammer for one dollar.

From books out of the Los Angeles Public Library, particularly Kenneth Henderson's *Handbook of American Mountaineering*, I learned that the proper method for using this gear was to drive the pitons into cracks and attach the rope to the ironware with the carabiners. In this way the leader created a safety system that provided security as he worked his way higher. A belayer fed the rope out and took it in as required. If the leader fell, it was the belayer's job to stop the fall by holding on to the rope. Because of the stretch in the rope (if it was nylon), the leader would fall a little more than twice the distance he was above his last piton. Manila hemp, lacking nylon's strength and elasticity, was not to be relied upon to stop a leader's fall. Therefore, before the invention of nylon ropes, the accepted climbing mantra was "The leader must not fall."

From instruction books I picked up other techniques such as rappelling, belaying, and prusiking and began to think I knew something about climbing. This was a mistake. I would later discover that learning to climb from books alone can be very dangerous.

Climbing whenever I could, I passed the rest of the summer reading science fiction stories and working at odd jobs until September when I returned to Thomas Starr King Junior High. Back in school I saw I was surrounded by potential climbing partners and right away tried to talk them into going climbing. Whenever I succeeded in convincing a fellow student to join me, I would grab my Manila hemp rope and climbing gear and hitchhike with my new partner into the San Gabriel Mountains searching for a suitable crag. Several times we visited an outcrop across the road from the Mount Waterman ski area. There we would practice for hours – rappelling, prusiking, and climbing around on the rotten granite. These baby steps on the little crag led to a solo adventure on a big rock just up the highway from Mount Waterman. I had discovered this 600-foot wall on an earlier hiking trip into the San Gabriels. Facing south, it rises out of a canyon on the desert side of the road between Mount Waterman and Crestline. The rock bears the same name as the peak it adjoins: Mount Williamson. Intent on exploring this cliff, I hitchhiked up the Angeles Crest Highway in October 1949, alone. My climbing partners from Starr King were game for just one outing. A mere taste of the experience had been enough for them. After that it was "No thanks!"

From the edge of the mountains in La Canada I got a ride with an older gentleman in a white pickup. He was going camping at Chilao Flat, about 10 miles short of my destination. "What's with the rope, young man?" he asked. I told him I was going to climb on a rock below the highway several miles past the Mount Waterman ski area. "Oh, I can take you right there. I'm not in a hurry, and it's only a little farther." I couldn't believe my good luck. I asked him to stop a mile short of Mount Williamson at a spot where I could more easily scramble down into the canyon and approach the cliff by following Little Rock Creek. His last words were, "Be careful." I assured him I would.

Descending into the shadows of the canyon, I reminded myself: You're here alone – watch your step. After reaching the streambed, I worked my way along the percolating brook toward the foot of the crag. Alder leaves made a bright red carpet on the forest floor while sunlight slanted through the thickly packed conifers. No leaf stirred. The only sound was the stream gurgling through the polished granite boulders. Deep in the canyon, I found the solitude strangely comforting, so different from the hubbub of the big city. With all this beauty, few people had been here. Few cared to be. I had found a balm for the spirit just over the hill from the vast noisy metropolis to the south.

Hiking up the streambed, I came to a spot where the creek emerged from beneath a giant boulder. I couldn't go that way. On my left a holdless cliff rose far overhead, while on my right was a low wall of granite. I could reach the top but there were no good holds to pull up on, and the wall itself had no holds at all. What to do here?

Then I noticed a small smooth pocket probably worn into the rock by a seasonal waterfall. If I could get a foot into it I would be high enough to get over the wall.

Suddenly I saw the answer. Pressing my hands against boulders on each side, I pushed strongly in opposite directions, levering my body up until I could put a foot into the pocket. After that, it was easy.

It was a simple maneuver I have often repeated, but this first time was inspiring because my mind and body were working together. I had solved a climbing problem! Seeing this moment as a portent of things to come, I realized in an illuminating instant how much I had to learn and how much climbing could teach me.

A hundred feet farther, a small wall of white granite rose above the streambed. Just the thing for practice climbing, I thought. I started up, carefully testing the rock – and myself – for weaknesses. The face lured me on, and I soon found myself on small holds 20 feet above a jumble of boulders. Since few people ventured into this canyon, a fall and a broken leg here might have been fatal. Mom was the only one who knew I was in the mountains somewhere, but she had no idea where. The tonic of danger was bracing, bringing me fully alert, fully alive. I zeroed in with total focus on each finger hold, each toe hold. Nothing else, for the moment, existed. In the canyon, alone, taking risks, I was happy.

From the top of the face, I could have scrambled down around the side of the rock. Instead, lured by the danger and by the total concentration required by the thin holds, I cautiously climbed back down the way I had come up. The intensity of that experience would keep me coming back for more.

I resumed my hike up the creek and soon reached the west edge of the Mount Williamson cliff. A short distance farther I came to a chimney that shot like an arrow straight up the left side of the face. This looks like the place, I thought, opting for the security of the groove over the featureless walls on either side. The crack was several feet wide, and I knew I could get inside and work my way up by pushing in opposite directions.

I entered the chimney and began working my way up using "scissors technique." With my back against one wall, I brought my legs up underneath me, knees bent and one foot braced against each wall. When I straightened my legs, I moved up a foot. Next, holding myself in place with hands pushing against opposite walls, I again brought my legs up. Gradually I scissored my way upward. Whenever the walls of the chimney closed in, I was forced to abandon the scissors technique and to thrash and struggle, worming my way up until I was past the narrow section. Although the crack required extremely strenuous maneuvering, I felt comfortable psychologically; I fancied I could stop myself if I slipped.

After several hundred feet, I found myself below a tough-looking bulge that would force me entirely out of the safety of the chimney. One slip here would take me all the way to the bottom.

Up to this point I had been uselessly trailing the rope tied to my waist. Now was the time to bring it into play. On a sling around one

Royal liebacking about halfway up the deep chimney on Mount Williamson Rock

shoulder, I carried three vertical pitons on my lone carabiner. Vertical pitons have the eye aligned with the blade. Horizontal pitons, in which the eye is at right angles to the blade, are more difficult to make and therefore more expensive. I could afford only verticals.

I unclipped one, found a little crack in the decomposed granite below the bulge, and hammered the vertical deep into it. Wanting to save my only carabiner for possible use higher up, I untied the rope from my body, passed the end through the eye of the piton, and tied it back around my waist. Reaching below the piton, I pulled up 30 feet of rope, tied an overhand loop, and clipped it to the rope around my waist with the carabiner. Now I felt much safer. If I fell, the rope running through the piton would hold me.

Or so I thought. Actually, if I had slipped while close to the piton, I would have fallen at least 15 feet (half the 30-foot loop). The sudden stop on the hemp rope would have been painful, to say the least. Even worse, if I had fallen from 15 feet above the piton I would have plunged 30 feet, and the full force would have come directly onto the piton. This would be a fall factor of 2, the worst possible. I didn't know it at the time, but I realize now that such a fall would almost certainly have broken the rope or pulled the piton out. Knowing nothing about fall factors, I imagined myself safeguarded by the piton with the Manila rope passed through the eye.

To pass the bulge I would need to "lieback." This technique was new to me, but my library books had described it in detail, and I was eager to put my book learning to the test. Digging my fingers into the crack, I started up. The rock was rounded, and there were no sharp edges. I pulled on the edge of the crack and braced my feet against the wall. One hand moved up, then a foot. My other hand moved up, then the other foot. Each move gained me only a few inches. The key to not falling lay in maintaining the tension between pulling with my arms and pushing with my feet. Higher and higher I struggled. This was it – real climbing! Just as the rope came taut between me and the piton, I pulled onto a ledge.

What luck! On the ledge I could let go with both hands to lengthen the loop. After doing so, I climbed another 10 feet to where the chimney closed in again. Here I stopped, braced securely against the chimney walls. Undoing the overhand loop, I pulled the rope through the eye of the piton, leaving the pin in place for discovery and possible retrieval by future climbers. I continued up the chimney over easier ground to the top. I was now poorer by one piton, but I had done a real climb on my own. My confidence grew. I felt ready for harder stuff.

A month later, before the winter snows arrived, I revisited Mount Williamson with my friend Tom Ackawie. I had gotten Tom into climbing and, unlike the others, he was eager for more. We hitch-hiked up with my ratty old rope and bits of gear, wearing tennis shoes, which worked well for both hiking and rock climbing. It took a lot of rides and several hours to get there, but we made it. From the highway, we followed my route down into the canyon and up Little Rock Creek to the base of the crag.

Looking for a new route, we passed the chimney and came to a section where the rock was less steep. Here we tied the ends of the Manila hemp rope around our waists and began the ascent. Being the more experienced climber, I did the leading, following gullies and corners that allowed me to sort of swim up by pushing on the sides in a modified chimney technique. The rock was rounded and decomposed, and there were few good holds. When I reached a belay spot, usually just a sort of sloping, curved hole, I called for Tom to come up and played at protecting him with the rope. I had no anchors. There were seams in the back of the gullies but no proper cracks into which I could pound one of our pitons. If Tom had fallen, he would have pulled me off my stance and both of us would have plunged to our deaths. Fortunately Tom was blessed with climbing talent. We eventually reached the top and lived to climb another day, but the adventure wasn't over.

As we regained the highway, the sun was low in the west and the hillsides were deep in shadow. Standing by the side of the road, thumbs in the air, we watched car after car zoom by, oblivious to our plight. We tried to look friendly and decent, smiling and erect, but the drivers were probably thinking, What are these two ragged, strange-looking kids doing hitchhiking up here, and what's that rope for? Eventually, to our immense relief, an 18-wheeler skidded to a halt on the side of the road, brakes screeching, gravel flying.

We ran over and threw open the door on the passenger side. The truck driver, a big fellow, beamed a friendly smile at us. He welcomed us aboard with "Hop in, boys!" but not quite as crisply as he might have. We soon saw why. He was in an expansive and generous mood, not due to any hopeful turn of events in his life, but because he had been drinking – apparently quite a bit. The cab reeked of alcohol. We should have said, "Thanks. We'll get out here," but we were afraid of insulting him. Also, it was late in the day, and we might not get another ride. We held on and hoped.

It was quite a ride as the big semi careened down the narrow, twisting Angeles Crest Highway. Wide-eyed with fear, we expected the truck to leave the road at each curve, plunging down the hillside and bursting into flame like they do in the movies. We breathed a sigh of relief when we hit the straightaway leading down into town out of the hills. We got out at Foothill Boulevard in La Canada where, happily, the drunken driver turned left while we went right. We were emotionally drained but happy to be alive. One of the problems with hitchhiking is you don't get to choose your chauffeur.

TO THE SCOUT JAMBOREE

Winter now intervened. I hung my climbing rope on a peg in my bedroom, often gazing fondly at it as I struggled with my schoolwork. Then, in the spring of 1950, the saga of the Rainbow Bus began. The creative mind of our Scoutmaster, Phil Bailey, came up with a bold enterprise that would further set us apart from all other troops: a tour of the country topped off by attending the National Jamboree in Valley Forge, Pennsylvania. The jamboree is an international Scout gathering that occurs every four years. Tens of thousands of Scouts come from all over the United States and from many countries around the world. The Scouts usually come individually or in small groups, but we would take the whole troop. It would be a mighty challenge to get all the way there and back again as one unit.

Phil's Los Angeles Police Department captain cajoled an executive at Greyhound Bus Lines into giving us a good price on a used vehicle. The result was a 37-passenger bus for only $4,000. (We would later learn why the bus was so affordable.) The LAPD came up with half of the purchase price. Our troop had to raise the other $2,000, a lot of money back then.

Assistant Scoutmaster Stan Stevenson thought of a highly original scheme for getting the two grand. We would sell pinyon nuts! This was a more daring idea than it first appeared, because these delicacies, otherwise known as pine nuts, were still in their shells. It was the very devil getting them out. When you got one, what did you have? A seed about 1/4 inch in length, suitable for salad garnish if you have dozens of them, but not of much use individually. Nevertheless, Stevenson was determined to pursue this method of raising the needed cash.

He was right. It worked! Mr. Stevenson's brilliant idea was based on the insight that, although people might not buy unshelled pine nuts for the nuts themselves, they would buy them to help a Scout troop pay for a bus to tour the United States. We took our little brown paper bags of pinyons, weighing about half a pound each, and went door to door, selling them for 75 cents a bag. Somehow we managed to sell thousands of bags and raised the $2,000, which these days would be well over $10,000.

At first I had difficulty seeing myself peddling unshelled pine nuts. Who was I to think I could sell anything? I was a climber and a hiker, an outdoorsman. After some initial success, however, my confidence grew. I began to see that what we were doing was an adventure. House to house I went, in my Scout uniform, up and down the streets near my home, knocking on doors. When the door opened, I would launch into my well-rehearsed spiel: "Hi. My name is Royal Robbins. I'm a member of Troop 127, the Rainbow Troop. We are trying to raise money so we can go to the National Scout Jamboree in Valley Forge, Pennsylvania, this summer. We need $2,000 to buy a bus to

Scout Jamboree program cover (1950)

take us there. So we are selling these pinyon nuts that are picked by Indians on their reservations. This helps the Indians too. The bags are 75 cents each. Would you like to buy some?" I was surprised at and gratified by how often the person at the door responded with "Yes," or "Sure, young man, give me three bags."

We might have sold packaged cookies or candy, but it wouldn't have been the same. We wouldn't have been as motivated. We believed in these pinyon nuts, and in our cause, and in helping those Indians. Also, it wouldn't have been the same for our customers. Even if what we were offering was worthless to some of them, it was unique and original. Today, as an adult, I buy my share of Girl Scout cookies but I would buy more and with more enthusiasm if they were baked by the Girl Scouts themselves.

We bought the bus and proceeded to paint it in the Rainbow colors – red, blue, gold, and black. Black? The paint company did not have purple paint and considered black a suitable substitute. The Purple Panthers rose as one voice: "No!" We wouldn't have black. The other patrols agreed. We had to get purple. Faced with customer resistance, the paint company went back to work and, by mixing colors, came up with "Automotive Purple" (later enshrined in their catalog as "Rainbow Troop Purple" and eventually a hot-rodder's delight). Thus we Panthers added our hue to the spectrum decorating the Rainbow Bus. We were ready to go!

The plan was to drive to Pennsylvania through the southern part of the United States and to come back through the north, in the process seeing a large part of America. After a little reflection, this idea was abandoned because we had a couple of black boys in the troop. It was deemed prudent to avoid any possibility of trouble in restaurants or other establishments due to their color. We would take the northern route both ways.

On the morning of June 24, 1950, we assembled in front of Los Angeles City Hall, spiffy in the new uniforms that were required for the jamboree. Our goal was to reach Valley Forge by the first of July and spend a week camping there. That of course included the 4th of July, so we would be in a historical place on a historical date. Much ado was made of our organization and our mission. The mayor, the chief of police, and a throng of newspaper reporters saw us off after a group picture in front of our magic carpet, the Rainbow Bus. All of this hoopla helped burn into our minds the significance of our adventure. Thirty-five Scouts were going, along with Scoutmaster Phil Bailey and Assistant Scoutmasters Stan Stevenson and Tom Canady. This would be the first time in Boy Scout history that an entire troop traveled across the country to attend a jamboree.

We planned to be gone a month and a half, including a week traveling to the jamboree, and a little over a week at Valley Forge, where George Washington, as commander of the colonial forces, spent a heroic winter in 1777-1778 during the Revolutionary War. The remaining four weeks would see us visiting many places across the United States as we returned west.

To cheers and applause, we drove off toward our destiny, excited by the prospect of weeks of new sights and experiences. It didn't take long for our dog of a bus to begin its habit of interrupting our progress by breaking down. Repeated malfunctions played havoc with our carefully laid plans of arrival and departure, with arrangements for housing and food, and with other prudent measures designed to ensure a trouble-free trip. Order was turned into chaos, a smooth drive into an open-ended adventure. Who knew what would happen next? Instead of staying in pre-selected campgrounds, we typically found ourselves bivouacking in city parks or high school gymnasiums. The *Los Angeles Times* kept a running account of our troubles, dubbing us the "Lost Battalion."

All these plans gone awry caused our leaders much frustration and anxiety, but to us Scouts it was simply a lark. As long as we had food and drink and a place to throw our sleeping bags, we were happy. I remember the trip as a total delight from beginning to end, with never a dull moment. A *Times* headline reported: "L.A. Scout Troop Enjoys Trip Despite Series of Breakdowns." An article on our being stranded in Santa Rosa, New Mexico, noted: "Scoutmaster Phil Bailey and his assistant, R. T. Canady, may be a little disturbed at the delay – but not the boys. They're having the time of their lives."

Arriving at the jamboree several days late, we quickly took our place among the 47,000 Scouts already there. Most of those attending were from the United States, but Scouts came from many other countries as well, including Iceland, Austria, and Chile, to name a few. The official literature emphasized the fundamental difference between the Communist youth movements and the world Scout movement. The Scouts had come voluntarily, whereas the gigantic rallies of the Communists were outwardly impressive but less so considering that attendance was mandatory.

My memories include a sea of tents, the morning salute and raising of our country's flag, open-air showers with walls but no roofs, hearty meals, hikes, the careful avoiding of the ubiquitous poison ivy, games, crafts, hobbies, historical tours, a speech by President

OMIGOSH, THIS IS ALMOST LIKE THE OLD ARMY ROUTINE

Citizen-News photo

Recipe for a picture. Take one Boy Scout Troop going en masse to the Scout Jamboree at Valley Forge, Pa. Add the special bus in which they travel. Throw in a pinch of the equipment that will be taken along. Then mix thoroughly the smallest scout on the tour with the biggest scout. Add a little authority to the latter. And "bingo"—you have the scene above with the poor little guy doing all the work while the big guy orders him around. Actually, this is all in fun as Gary Marx, 11½, of 1976 N. Berendo St., follows directions of Troop Quartermaster Larry Sparks. The Rainbow Troop, sponsored by the L.A. Police Dept., is the only local troop going, in its entirety, to the Jamboree. Troop leaves Sunday and will return to L.A., July 29.

Rainbow Bus newspaper photo

Troop 127 assembled in front of their bus

Truman, and just lounging about. International trade flourished. Scouts brought marbles, trinkets, medals, stamps, cards, and other items from around the world to barter. Countless exchanges of these valuables were accompanied by a sharing of experience and of points of view.

Shortly after arriving I wrote home:

Dear Mom, We just got in this morning, because the bus broke down three times and we had to get a new motor once. But don't worry because we have had a lot of fun. I think I might be able to make Life Scout by the next court of honor. I am working on Forestry [merit badge] every chance I get. The patrol I am in was selected as the best patrol and as a reward we get to eat with Chief Scout of America. Well I can't think of anything else to say except I wanted to ask you if you can send me some more money? Thanks, Love, Royal.

The great convention finally came to an end with fireworks and fanfare, and we loaded the Rainbow Bus and headed for Washington, D.C., and its historic monuments. We were awed by the statue of Lincoln brooding over the burdens of keeping our nation together in the crisis of the Civil War. We climbed to the top of the obelisk built as a memorial to our first president. Then the bus broke down again, this time in front of the headquarters of the Washington Redskins football team. The *Los Angeles Times* commented: "Bus Trouble Again Hits Scout Troop."

Our bus repaired, we proceeded to Philadelphia, Annapolis, New York, West Point, and Boston, where we saw many things, some historic, some modern. We got soaked in a boat ride under Niagara Falls, went into Canada, and then passed through Detroit and Chicago on our way back west. A common experience, both going and coming, was meeting warm and friendly people eager to extend a helping hand. It didn't hurt that we were sponsored by the Los Angeles Police Department. The brotherhood of the thin blue line repeatedly came to our rescue in providing things like lodging or even a police escort through a busy town when we were running behind due to breakdowns.

We were rolling across the plains of South Dakota when Dennis Weiner, one of my fellow Scouts, began to complain of severe pains in his stomach. Being a long way from any hospital, we stopped at a farmhouse to call for help. By a tremendous stroke of luck or divine grace, the house was owned by a doctor and his wife. The husband was out visiting patients, but the wife's brother, also a doctor, happened to be visiting. He diagnosed the condition as acute appendicitis, requiring an immediate operation. Fortunately, there was a little operating room in the house. Designed for minor emergencies, it would have to do. The operation was a success; Dennis would be OK. After camping on the farm that night we continued our trek the next day, leaving the convalescent behind, as there was no room for him to stretch out in the bus. Mr. Canady stayed with Dennis until he was well enough to travel, and together they flew back to Los Angeles.

We continued across South Dakota to a scenic area known as the Badlands. This barren earth, parched and lacerated with a maze of arroyos, gullies, and ravines, may have looked bad to farmers, but to us boys, it was "goodlands," a place where one could have adventures. I was immediately intrigued.

Our multihued hound of a bus lurched to a stop at a parking area on the edge of the Badlands: lunch time. Piling onto the tarmac, we found ourselves gazing over a landscape molded through the millennia by wind and rain and now silently awaiting the next flash flood. We saw no trees or even wildflowers. The only signs of life were occasional tufts of grass nestled in protective hollows. On the north side of the parking lot, a serpentine gully wound downward, seductive with the promise of hidden treasure.

While the rest of the troop enjoyed lunch, I suggested to a few boys of my ilk that we pop down and "have a look around the corner." We slipped away. One corner led to another, as curiosity pulled us, enchanted, deeper and deeper into a magical little canyon kingdom. This was the best part of the entire trip. The mysteries of the maze drew us on and on, down the snaking ravine. Suddenly we realized how much time had passed. Oops – we were in trouble! Reluctantly tearing ourselves away from the next tantalizing revelation, we turned around and raced back to the parking area.

Too late! There stood the bus, all alone on the asphalt, shining in the brilliant sunlight, primed to depart. All the Scouts were on board, ready to go, all, that is, except for our delinquent band of four. It was too late to sneak in and mingle with our mates. We stood out like prodigal sons, shuffling up to the bus door where our Scout leaders stood, arms across their chests, glaring. The grim looks were no joke, and they gave us a well-deserved tongue-lashing. I received the brunt of the sermon, directly from Mr. Bailey. He somehow knew I was the ringleader. Chastened, I apologized: "I'm sorry, Mr. Bailey. I won't do it again." I really meant it at the time, though, as we shall see, I would find it hard to repress the instinct to seek adventure.

We arrived back in Los Angeles several days later than had been planned, which was all the better from the point of view of us boys. Parents were on hand to pick us up. There was a lot of hugging, whooping, and laughter. We would carry the wonder and joy of that 7,000-mile adventure through the rest of our lives.

A PRICELESS LESSON

After we returned from the Rainbow Bus journey, I resumed my search for places to climb, in the process rediscovering Stoney Point. This area had caught my fancy several years earlier during one of our train-hopping escapades. On that occasion, as we were passing through the San Fernando Valley one spring day, our freight had pulled onto a side track next to a hill of sandstone outcrops. This, I later learned, was Stoney Point. Curious about this mysterious land of rocks, we explored the intriguing cliffs for a couple of hours, knowing our train wouldn't depart until another had passed on the main rail. Then when we heard a train thundering below, we ran down and got into our boxcar, but not until I had made a mental note of the approximate location in case we should ever want to come back.

In early September 1950, after I had entered high school, I remembered that train ride and those sandstone outcrops. Checking a street map of the San Fernando Valley, I noted a junction of a railroad track and Topanga Canyon Boulevard just north of the small town of Chatsworth. Maybe that was it. I hitchhiked out one Saturday morning to see what I could discover. Sure enough, there it was; I recognized it instantly. My ride deposited me on the west side, and

I found a trail up the south slopes that took me to the top where I could look down on the railroad tracks to the northeast. I scrambled all over Stoney, investigating its secrets, laying plans for future visits.

The top was about 300 feet above the road. Trails on the west led up through brush to a band of 100-foot cliffs broken occasionally by cracks or deep chimneys. Along these trails poison oak peeked out from among the other bushes, but with caution the rash-producing leaves could be avoided. It was harder to avoid the broken glass and graffiti scrawled on the rock surfaces. Stoney was part of the great outdoors, but it paid the price for being close to urban centers. Atop the cliffs on the west side sat a single large boulder like a king on his throne. Another prominent boulder stood alone on the flat ground near the road. On top of this 20-foot rock I found some large bolts, evidence that "real" climbers had been there.

All in all, Stoney looked like a prize discovery – highly accessible and an excellent place to practice. It was a lot closer than Mount Williamson, and one could climb here in the winter months when snow blanketed the San Gabriels. I would soon return with rope and pitons.

That same month, during one of my weekly visits to the Los Angeles Public Library, I came across *High Conquest*, an intriguing history of mountaineering by James Ramsey Ullman. This book, with its philosophy of adventure, changed my life. Climbing was more than fun and outdoor action. True conquest was not of the physical mountains rising from the surface of our planet, but rather of the inner mountains of the soul. *Those* were the mountains worth conquering.

After the epiphany of *High Conquest*, I went climbing as often as possible. I didn't wait for weekends. Right after school I grabbed my

Royal liebacking at Stoney Point (age 15)

equipment and thumbed my way to Stoney Point. I must have looked a sight, on the busy Los Angeles and San Fernando Valley streets, rope over one shoulder, pitons and carabiners clipped to a sling over the other. Sometimes I had trouble getting rides and arrived at the rock with only a half hour to climb before I had to start hitchhiking home. Getting there and back sometimes was the whole adventure. Occasionally I was able to cajole a fellow student into joining me, but I never could get the same friend to go twice. Maybe they simply had a realistic view of the risks involved and were happy to escape alive.

After arriving at Stoney, my partner and I would boulder for a while to warm up. Then we attacked longer routes with a safety line from above. Finally, I would lead climbs, starting from the base and using pitons for protection. My natural ease on the rock, compared to my companion's nervousness, led to a level of self-confidence perilously close to arrogance. I began to feel I couldn't fall. Then a lightning bolt of reality shocked me into a new humility.

I was with a companion who had never climbed before. I don't remember his name. We had hitched rides to Chatsworth one Saturday morning in late September 1950. Our last ride stopped by Stoney on Topanga Canyon Boulevard. Thanking the driver, we descended onto the gravel flats near Little Rock #1 and Little Rock #1/2, the two boulders closest to the road. After practicing on these rocks for an hour, we hiked up the trail about 200 feet, roped up, and climbed an easy crack near the left side of the big west face. That was a confidence builder for my companion and he began to relax. I coiled the rope and we wandered along the summit plateau to the east side of Stoney, where we found ourselves atop a sharp cliff about 50 feet high. I had climbed several routes here already and was intent on a new line near its southern edge.

We scrambled down through brush to the bottom of the south end of the wall and walked north 50 feet. This was the spot. Hints of ledges led up and right to a small stance 25 feet above the boulder-strewn ground. I drew the piton hammer from my pack, slipped it into my holster, and threw around my shoulder a sling with half a dozen pitons and carabiners. After tying in, I gave my partner instructions on rope handling and belaying. I hadn't bothered to do so on the easy route on the west side, but this was going to be more serious.

I started up, climbing free to the small stance. Here the rock steepened and became holdless, but a crack split the wall above. My plan was to drive pitons into that crack and use them to move upward. The books called this "tension climbing." After placing a piton I would clip my rope to it with a carabiner and have my belayer hold me on "tension," while I reached up and placed a higher piton. From my book learning I knew the method was to insert a piton 1/2 to 2/3 of its length into a crack and then hammer it in up to the eye. A clear and rising pinging sound indicated a solid placement. To further test the peg, I could tap it several times. If the hammer rebounded with a healthy spring, the placement was probably solid.

I did these things, and the piton passed the tests. What should I do next? What I should have done was climb back down and vigorously pull on the piton by jumping from the safety of a ledge close to the ground. Or I could have driven another piton for additional protection, but I didn't yet understand the principle of redundancy.

Looking up at the smooth wall, aware of the air beneath me, I suddenly felt afraid. What was I getting into? I was too green to realize my fear was justified. I thought it was cowardice, and that disgusted me – I wouldn't give in. My tests indicated a solid piton. A *real* climber wouldn't be afraid to use it.

I clipped a carabiner to the piton and attached my rope. Asking my belayer to hold me on tension, I leaned back, applying my full weight to the peg. It instantly popped out of the crack. Tumbling over backward, I crashed down onto the rocks at the base of the cliff. The pain was overwhelming. I couldn't believe I had actually fallen. As I writhed in agony among the boulders, I swore to myself I would never go climbing again. Nothing was worth this!

My unfortunate partner certainly would never climb again. He stared at me in disbelief. I had been whole a few moments earlier, but here I was before him – broken and moaning. Everything hurt, but I was conscious of even more severe pain in my right ankle and left wrist. At least I could still walk, sort of. We got our equipment together, and leaning on my friend, I hobbled out to the road.

Luckily we got a ride right away from a kind lady who was driving her father into Los Angeles. She could see I'd had an accident. She was sympathetic, but soon asked, "Do your mother and father know what you are doing?" I explained I didn't have a father and that, yes, Mom let me do it. I didn't elaborate on the fact that Mom realized she never could have stopped me anyway and therefore didn't even try, though I was sure she did a lot of praying.

This splendid and gracious lady went out of her way to drive me all the way home so I could avoid further hitchhiking and get to a doctor as soon as possible. She probably told my mother it might be a good idea if I didn't climb anymore, though Mom never mentioned the means of climbing, and he must be able to take in the rope very slowly against a strong pull. By leaning out against the tension of the rope, the climber can make his feet stick even on vertical faces (Figure 41). By this means it is possible to climb slowly upward if the second man can at the same time take in some rope. When the level of the piton is reached, the process must be repeated with another piton placed higher up. It is also possible to use this same technique for resting even on an ordinary climb by warning the second man to hold the rope firmly and then leaning out against it, thus resting the arms and legs.

The *double rope technique* is the ultimate refinement of rope tension climbing. It permits absolutely smooth and holdless faces and slabs to be climbed, provided only that cracks for pitons can be found. The leader ties on with two ropes, one descending from the right and the other from the left hip. If these ropes are different in type or size, it helps prevent confusion. By pulling on one rope until the leader reaches the piton and can place the second rope in a higher piton and then pulling on the second rope, the second man can enable the leader to

Figure 41. Rope tension climbing — driving pitons

Tension climbing, from Handbook of American Mountaineering, by Henderson

it. Mom probably hoped the accident would teach me
doctor told me I had a badly sprained ankle and a bro
put a cast on my left arm, and the healing began. After
pain from the accident became a distant memory an
again turned to climbing.

Here I was, stuck in the drab, humdrum city, while in my mind
the hills glittered, calling me back. Realizing how much climbing
meant to me, I renounced my vow never to climb again. Nothing
came close to the joy I felt moving over rock, whether effortlessly or
fighting for every inch. One setback couldn't destroy my desire. I was
made for climbing. I had to go back.

Instead of giving up, I would learn from my mishap. I knew well
enough that the rock had not caused my fall. The accident was the
result of ignorance and lack of judgment. Words from a book were
not enough. I needed to take upon myself the responsibility to think
through what I was doing. I had to become a hardheaded realist. My
life was in my own hands; it was up to me to take good care of it.

Years later I read Edward Whymper's famous lines and realized
their truth:

> *Climb if you will, but remember that courage and strength are
> naught without prudence and that a momentary negligence may
> destroy the happiness of a lifetime. Do nothing in haste; look
> well to each step; and from the beginning think what may be
> the end.*

REAL CLIMBERS

In October 1950, two weeks after my accident, I hitchhiked to Stoney Point. A boy with his arm in a cast gets rides more easily, and I soon found myself gazing down from the road at Little Rock #1. I was astonished to see a couple dozen adults with ropes, rugged climbing clothing, and jaunty alpine hats. Real climbers! They were belaying, rappelling, and climbing on Stoney's premium boulder.

I stood there awhile, watching them, unsure of my next move. Then, suppressing excitement and trying to act casual, I wandered down to the group of strangers. I must have appeared a peculiar specimen, a skinny kid with my arm in a cast and a ratty hemp rope over one shoulder. Who did I think I was? If they wondered, they didn't ask. They were friendly and welcoming.

"Who are *you*?" I innocently blurted out.

"We're from the Sierra Club," a lady in climbing garb cheerfully responded. "We're here to practice rock climbing. Want to join us?"

Of course I did! Real climbers – the only ones I had ever seen except for the Scout leaders on Fin Dome. I could scarcely believe my ears. This was a dream come true. These were real mountaineers and maybe I could be one of them!

They were members of the Rock Climbing Section (RCS) of the Los Angeles Chapter of the Sierra Club. Friendly and encouraging, they seemed the best people I had ever met. I shyly asked if I could try a climb. A serious-looking, strongly built man wearing an alpine hat offered me the end of a rope. I passed it around my waist, tied a bowline backed up with two half-hitches, and offered it to his inspection. To my immense relief, he smiled and nodded OK. Now I was part of the group.

I surprised them – and myself – by getting up five of the six routes on the boulder. One problem that defied my best efforts lay in a niche on the north side of the practice rock. It required a push hold I couldn't manage with my left arm in a cast. On the other routes I could cling to the pull holds with my fingers sticking out of the cast. My broken bones had already fused together in just two weeks. A few days later I had the cast removed.

It didn't hurt my estimation of this group that one of them, Jim Gorin, climbed with only one leg. Not only that, he climbed well. He cheerfully hopped and mantled his way up the routes on Little Rock #1. Laughter sprang spontaneously from these Sierra Clubbers, but underlying the joy was a high level of alertness. They were attentive to belays, they double-checked the anchors, and everyone climbed with total concentration on this 20-foot rock. It was as if they were preparing for big tests in the real mountains, which in fact they were.

In my chance falling-in with these Sierra Club rock climbers, I had stepped into a new world. At last I had discovered true companions in the vertical endeavor. No longer would I be forced to solo or compel reluctant schoolmates to come along to belay. I'd found mentors and leaders whose passion for climbing matched my own.

In December I attended the RCS annual meeting at Boos Brothers Cafeteria in downtown Los Angeles. We were in a separate room where Kodachrome slides could be projected onto a large screen. I was in heaven, surrounded by climbers all talking about nothing but climbing! This was more like it! Why talk about anything else? Then came the slides – real climbing up real rocks and mountains. There was a southern California crag called Mount Pacifico, and some shots of climbing at Stoney Point. There was the High Sierra – Mount

Whitney and the Palisades. There were pictures of the Royal Arches and Cathedral Spires in Yosemite Valley. There was even a 1,000-foot granite cliff right here in southern California – Tahquitz Rock. I couldn't wait to get there, but that would have to be next summer. Tahquitz was above the snow line, and before I was allowed on a Club climb at Tahquitz, I would have to attend at least three practice climbs at places like Stoney Point and Mount Pacifico, and pass the safety test.

The RCS quieted down during the winter. Many of its members also belonged to the Ski Mountaineers Section, and this time of year they put on their boards for the white stuff. In the spring the RCS resumed outings at Stoney Point.

I was there every time.

CHAPTER VI

Breaking Free

DOMESTIC AFFAIRS

Back in the late summer of 1950, before my encounter with the RCS, I had eagerly enrolled in John Marshall High School. High school, at last! This had to be an improvement on Thomas Starr King. After all, high school was for kids who were nearly adults. Alas, John Marshall was even worse than junior high – pettier, crueler, even tougher academically. I was out of my element. Nevertheless, I struggled on, vaguely hoping to be transformed by a magic wand into someone who could cope.

At that time we were still living on Commonwealth Avenue. In November, Mom, Penny, and I left our communal home and moved over the hill to Hyperion Avenue. Mom was now making enough money as a cosmetician to afford a place of our own. We said goodbye to our relatives, not that we wouldn't be seeing them again, and often, but it was goodbye to daily living together. We had formed a rich kinship, born of necessity, nurtured by imagination, and producing harmony and good will. The experience of living with all those people has stayed with me ever since as a lesson in making do. By pooling our resources, we had plenty. Separately, we would have been hard pressed.

OUTDOOR ADVENTURE WITH TROOP 121

During our six-week Rainbow Bus tour, a fateful change had occurred in the leadership of the Los Angeles Police Department. A new chief of police decreed that the Boy Scouts were not a proper part of the mission of the force. The result, later in the year, was the disbanding of 17 LAPD-sponsored Scout troops. The Rainbow Troop did not escape the axe and ceased to exist in December 1950.

In high school I'd had the good fortune to make friends with a fellow student, Bill Derr, who became a close friend and climbing partner. Tall, confident, possessing a lively sense of humor, Bill had a taste for outdoor action that rivaled my own. Learning that I was a climber and had just left the Scouts, he suggested I join him in Troop 121 where climbing was a regular activity. Troop 121 was different from the Rainbow Troop and, I am sure, different from every other troop in Los Angeles. I had the incredibly good luck of joining two of the most remarkable Scouting units in Los Angeles.

If the main thrust of the Rainbow Troop was adventure in general, the driving spirit in Troop 121 was specifically *outdoor* adventure. Besides hiking and camping, they climbed mountains and skied. Scoutmaster Al Wilkes inspired the troop's quest for open-air action. Quick, cheerful, ever optimistic, Al was afire with love for the out-of-doors. He had keen, chiseled features and eyes with hawklike intensity. When he smiled or laughed, which was often, his eyes lost their raptor quality and twinkled with childlike eagerness. Al's enthusiasm captivated us boys. He was a natural leader.

When I joined Troop 121 in January 1951, they were laying plans for a June assault on the North Face of Mount San Jacinto, a granite peak rising above the desert near Palm Springs, 100 miles east of Los Angeles. At 10,804 feet, San Jacinto is not high by western U.S. standards. Indeed, Mount San Gorgonio, standing in proud rivalry just across the desert, rises 700 feet higher. Nevertheless, San Jack, as we came to know it, boasts one of the steepest 8,000-foot escarpments in the United States. The ascent of this wall is mostly high-angle hiking, but there are steep sections requiring a rope for safety.

Al got the idea of climbing the North Face after hiking to the top of San Jacinto from Idyllwild, a small town in a broad valley on the gentle western slope. Looking down those thousands of feet at the desert floor, he conceived the perfect adventure for the members of Troop 121 seeking a big outdoor challenge. As soon as I joined, I counted myself among that group.

This was to be the troop's third attempt on the face. The first, two years earlier, had ended when the climbers gave up in exhaustion. They hadn't brought salt tablets, and the inevitable dehydration resulted in cramps, nausea, and a strange malady Al diagnosed as "flaking out."

An accident doomed the second attempt. Alan English, one of the Scouts on that trip, remembers it:

> "We had climbed almost halfway up the face, at least 3,000 feet. We had stopped for lunch at a pool along Snow Creek. Darrel Fowler went for a drink from the stream when he caught his foot and fell backwards into the pool. His leg was badly broken. We had to carry him down."

> "We cut down a couple of saplings and made a sort of stretcher with shirts and parkas. Then we started. It was awful. Poor Fowler screamed with pain all the way down. We couldn't help jostling him, and he was in terrific pain even when we were still. It was brutal with that stretcher. It was bad enough with

just the weight and the steep mountainside, but the screaming was unnerving. By nightfall we had got about halfway down."

Al Wilkes adds:

"I sent the two oldest boys on down for help, through the darkness and mostly without a trail. By the time they got to a telephone it was dawn, and without sleep they led a couple of sheriff's men back up to our camp some 2,000 feet higher. The two sheriff's team members were pooped from the fast climb so some of our guys helped carry Fowler the rest of the way down."

These failed attempts, in my mind, added value to the enterprise. This was real: boys climbing serious mountains like grown men. Two tries and twice soundly defeated, yet here they were laying plans for another attempt. This was not make-believe. I had entered a fellowship of high adventure.

For five long months, with eager anticipation, I thought about the coming encounter with the big mountain near Palm Springs. Finally, one Friday afternoon at the end of spring 1951, we drove out of Los Angeles for the third attempt. Cruising through open country, we reached Redlands and then Banning, where the grass of the Los Angeles basin gives way to sand and cactus. We stopped for hamburgers, fries, and Cokes at a Banning drive-in, then resumed our drive along the highway toward Palm Springs, soon finding ourselves in the shadow of San Jacinto. A dirt road took us up a wash to granite cliffs and a lively brook, where we spent the night at about 3,000 feet. The stream that sang in our ears as we lay in our sleeping bags was Snow

Creek, sparkling down from high on the North Face to vanish in the hot sands of the desert. This creek would be our friend and guide for the next two days, leading us to the alpine upper reaches.

We arose at dawn and, after a quick breakfast of milk and cinnamon rolls, we were on our way. It was a perfectly clear June day, warm but not hot, and as we gained altitude, the refreshing coolness of the mountain asserted itself. By late afternoon we reached the 8,000-foot level – less than 3,000 feet to go. Here we found a perfect campsite right next to Snow Creek and just below a small cliff of white granite.

In the cool shadows of late afternoon, as my fellow Scouts busied themselves with camp chores, I began silently soloing the rock face above. I couldn't resist the lure of steep rock. My Scoutmaster glanced up to see me clinging to small holds 20 feet above the ground. He doubtless had visions of another boy being carried down the mountain with a broken leg, or worse. I felt secure but it must have looked highly risky to Mr. Wilkes. Al was always soft-spoken and gentle toward his Scouts, but this time, after commanding me to get down, he let me know in very strong terms that I was not to go climbing around without a rope!

Embarrassed at being singled out for unscoutlike behavior, I apologized, as I had in the Badlands incident, and promised that I wouldn't do it again. I was eager to get back into the good graces of my leader and idol. After chewing me out, Al gave the incident no more thought. We were friends again. Life returned to normal.

We cooked, ate dinner, and then slipped into our sleeping bags as night closed round. Lying on my back, I looked up at countless stars sparkling brightly in a deep black sky. I had rarely noticed them

Troop 121 boys on top of San Jacinto (Scoutmaster Al Wilkes at top of photo, Royal at far right)
Photo: Jim Brigham

North Face of San Jacinto with Snow Creek

through the lights and thick atmosphere of the city. Sitting up, I peered down at the desert floor to see the tiny headlights of cars passing along the highway. Lights from homes and businesses also glittered through the darkness. Even after 5,000 feet of climbing, we hadn't quite escaped the trappings of the world down there. At last, drowsy after a long and demanding day, I joined my fellow Scouts in slumberland.

We arose in the cool dawn to a cloudless sky, refreshed by a good night's sleep. After a quick breakfast of cereal and milk, we started up, occasionally using a rope for safety on steep sections, but mostly hiking and scrambling up the remaining 2,800 feet. We were on top before noon, glowing with the pride of accomplishment. For the first time since Fin Dome I enjoyed the ritual summit handshake.

Exhilarated, we took in the scenery in big gulps of wide-eyed wonder. Far, far below us lay the flat, scorched desert. To the north, the vast bulk of Mount San Gorgonio rose in giant swells. Turning to the southwest, we could make out, in the mountain valley below, the little town of Idyllwild. Above it stood a magnificent white pillar, Tahquitz Rock. At the time I had no inkling of the major role this crag would play in my life, but there was something undeniably attractive about the way it towered above the trees. Off to the northwest, the landscape was obliterated by the haze and smog drifting in from the L.A. basin. It was good to be up here, in our own little world atop San Jacinto. We were, in a way, close to Los Angeles, with its teeming millions. Yet in other ways, in our surroundings of thin air and conifers and granite, and in our interior landscape of joy and wonder, we were far, so very far, from the heart of the city.

Summits are the high points of life, but you can't stay on top forever. We started down, cautiously wending our way toward the desert floor. The story of Fowler's broken leg and his ordeal was vivid in our minds, so we gave each step concentration and care. The descent took countless steps, but we finally made it, arriving in the late afternoon at the cars parked next to Snow Creek. We were exhausted but happy. Smiles beamed through the dust on our haggard faces. We had climbed the North Face of San Jacinto! And we got back down in one piece.

I passed the rest of the summer climbing whenever I could, sometimes on my own, but often on outings with the RCS. Over the Labor Day weekend I was part of an RCS team that climbed Mount Williamson, a 14,000-foot peak in the Sierra Nevada.

GOODBYE TO SCHOOL

In September 1951 I reluctantly resumed my studies at John Marshall High School. Climbing had given my spirit wings. It was as if my flying dreams had come true. But sitting in the classroom was like being a prisoner in a world I didn't understand. All I knew was that in this world I was a failure.

There was a moment of hope early in the semester. I was repeating English class because my marks had been so bad the previous year. The modest success of my first two essays was briefly encouraging. The teacher kindly gave me topics I could relate to. The subject of the first paper was "What I Did Last Summer." Of course, what I mostly did was climb, so I described our ascent of the Sierran giant, Mount

Williamson. The B+ I got on that paper was a summit in my school life. The other subject, "The Sport I Like Best," was a natural for me. I received a B on that essay. Looking at it today, I realize the teacher was grading softly. An excerpt:

Unlike must people think, Mountianeering is not a sport for muscle men, it requires more intelligience than any out-door sport, and therefore a mountian is not only a challange to the agilty, strength and endurance of a man, but also to his intelligience and injinuity.

The essay didn't explain how someone smart enough to climb was so poor at spelling.

I couldn't earn even a C in any other class, and socially I seemed to be straight F. What was wrong with me? Why couldn't I get a girlfriend? And then there were the team sports, but hitting a baseball or sinking a basketball was beyond me. We were introduced to badminton, a one-on-one sport that brought out my competitive instinct. Badminton was fun, and I won more than my share of games, but it was not a regular part of the PE curriculum. So it was dropped.

When they took away the only school sport I was any good at, I sought solace in the mountains. In October Bill Derr and I hitchhiked up into the San Gabriels to climb on the rock at our own Mount Williamson. We had gotten a ride to the junction of the Angeles Forest and Angeles Crest Highways and there, across from a Forest Service ranger station, we stuck out our thumbs. A few minutes later a 1949 Mercury station wagon pulled over, and we hopped aboard. The driver, whose name was Lynn Newcomb, owned a ski area, Mount Waterman, farther up the highway. He also owned a restaurant near

Chilao Flat called Newcomb's Inn. If we wanted to work at his ski area, he told us, there might be openings in the coming winter.

Skiing? That was a new idea, something I had never tried before. Like climbing, it was a risky outdoor sport – back in those days there were no release bindings. I was intrigued. The very next month I went with Troop 121 on a Thanksgiving ski trip to Sequoia National Park. There was a small ski area with rope tows. It was pretty exciting strapping on those long boards for the first time. If any instruction on how to do it was given, I didn't listen. I just took off and did whatever worked. We skied three days, and I discovered a new passion. It was scary, thrilling, and dangerous! And fast. I blasted down the hill, again and again, pushing myself to the limit, and occasionally out of control. On the last run of the last day, in a fit of excessive exuberance, I crashed and sprained my ankle. It didn't matter. I had missed no skiing.

My ankle healed quickly, and at the beginning of December, Bill Derr and I drove up in his car to apply for jobs at Mount Waterman. We were hired to work at the ski area on weekends – I was put in charge of a rope tow on the gentle slopes at the top of the mountain. I learned to ski and somehow survived many falls. It was an exhilarating escape from Los Angeles and the weekly drudgery of schoolwork.

That December a huge storm dropped an alarming amount of snow. Up on the Angeles Crest Highway a snowplow was reported missing and was feared buried in an avalanche. Six of us slogged up the highway on skis, searching for the plow. This might have been a very dangerous thing for us to do, but we felt like heroes. It all ended well; the plow had gotten past the avalanche section and was safe.

Back in school, the bright flame that skiing had kindled in my spirit was snuffed out, and during the week life again looked black. I took a perverse pleasure in wallowing in a bog of self-pity. Returning home from school each afternoon brought no relief. I passed the rest of the day and evening telling myself how essentially stupid and worthless I was. Again and again I raked myself over the soul-frying coals of inadequacy. I wouldn't dare think, much less express, such vile thoughts about anyone else. Mercilessly, I took pen and paper and wrote out the most malicious and hurtful things I could think to say about myself. Like a character out of Dostoevsky, I was "a wretch, wretch, wretch, wretch!" If only I were good at something, if only I were smarter, everything would be all right. My grades in school proved I was a failure. Obsessed with despair, I was going in the same direction as my stepfather, but instead of alcohol, I was being poisoned with self-hatred.

Near the end of the school year, in May 1952, some sane part of myself, a deeply healthy element of my soul, demanded a hearing. It declared this mental and emotional flagellation a disease. I needed to stop thinking this way. I saw that school, with its opportunities for invidious comparisons, simply fed the illness. It was different outdoors. In the mountains I didn't carry this monstrous backpack of mental rubbish. If school was that bad for me, then to hell with it! I had a choice. I could quit! Summer vacation was coming soon; after that, I would not return. With that thought, an immense burden fell from my shoulders. I was free!

About this time, Bill Derr surprised me by talking about leaving school. He was a good student but felt that high school was an anchor tying him down, keeping him from exploring. It was time to move on. During the summer we discussed quitting high school and decided to leave together. But where would we go and what would we do?

Suddenly, Bill started up, eyes widening with enthusiasm: "Hey, wait a minute. We can go up and work full time at Mount Waterman!" Yes, I thought. That's the answer. I can work and live in my beloved mountains.

I talked it over with Mom. She was dismayed at first, but quickly realized opposition would only harden my headstrong resolve. She tried to keep alive in me the idea of a high school diploma: "You can always finish school later." I had no intention of doing so, but I didn't say it; I didn't want to add to her disappointment.

We went up to see Lynn. "OK, fellows. You're on. I'll see you November first."

And so it happened. We worked harder that winter at Mount Waterman than we ever had at school, but we didn't notice because our hearts were in it. The future lay before us as a magnificent adventure: we could ski all winter and climb all summer and there was no schoolwork!

For me, life had begun anew. I poured myself into each fresh possibility, but especially into climbing. I spent years developing my climbing skills and sense of self-mastery. As time passed, my concept of what was possible kept expanding. Eventually, in 1963, my thoughts turned to the overhanging face of the Leaning Tower, and to the challenge of climbing it alone.

CHAPTER VII

Return to the Realm

Belay seat bivouac

TOPPING OUT

It's now late afternoon of my third day on the West Face of the Leaning Tower. Since morning I've climbed three overhanging pitches – leading, rappelling, cleaning, and hauling each one. I've struggled all day – pitoning up cracks, clipping to bolts, dangling in space.

Rain still pelts Yosemite Valley and its cliffs, but the lean of the Tower has kept me dry. Streaks of icy water seep down the wall and drip off the overhangs. Everything is damp and cold, but I'm warm from fighting for every vertical inch. Only one major obstacle, a sharp triangular roof, stands between me and the summit, less than 300 feet away. Tomorrow, after I climb that roof, I'll be close to victory.

It seems an age since that first morning when, gripped by fear and filled with doubt, I fought back a desire to give up. Nevertheless, like Ahab, I stayed steadfast to my mad purpose. From that uncertain beginning my confidence has soared with every vertical foot gained. Now I find myself loving the steepness, feeling at home in the realm of the overhang.

With darkness fast approaching, it's time to prepare for the night. The only ledge is upside down – the overhang directly above me – so I'll need to rig a hanging bivouac. I'm anchored to two bolts placed by the first ascent party. They look solid, but searching for a little extra security, I reach up, drive a piton into the crack above, and clip in. It will help me sleep better.

Next I draw from the top of my pack a belay seat of ripstop nylon. It's a neat little item, nearly weightless, that Liz designed and sewed together for me. Bless her. With this gadget I can avoid a sleepless night standing in slings. Attaching each end loop to a bolt, I make a comfortable seat, resting my feet in the aid slings to take pressure off my thighs.

Then I sort my bivouac equipment. Lacking a ledge to serve as a table, I clip every item I draw from my haul bag to one of my anchors. The rest of my supplies stay jumbled together in the sack. Naturally whatever I want is always at the bottom; why can't it ever be on top? Forced to search again and again, deep in the bag, for this item or that, I swear that next time I'll make sure every piece of gear or food can be clipped to a carabiner outside the sack.

At last I finish sorting, and then enjoy the pure pleasure of reaching down and loosening the laces on my tight shoes. It would be even better to take them off and give my poor aching feet some relief, but that's too risky. I might get to the top of the Tower, but the prospect of descending to the Valley in socks makes me shudder.

Or maybe I'm shivering because the temperature is hovering near the freezing point. Now that I am no longer climbing, the chill is seeping through my wool sweater. I carefully pull my Jamet jacket from the pack and slip my arms into its puffy sleeves. These French down jackets – super light, super warm – sure beat sweaters. Now that I'm cozy I could just conk out, but I know I should eat something to keep up my strength for that tough roof above.

So I rummage again through the pack. Pulling out the bag of gorp, I munch a handful. That does it; now I know why they call bits of food before a meal "appetizers." After more searching, I happen onto the salami and cheese and some stale bread rolls. Oh no, not more of that stuff! Then I remember the tuna. Digging deeper into the bag, I come across the little can I'd casually tossed in back at Camp 4. It was meant to top off a summit celebration, but I've slaved away for days and victory is in sight. Dammit! I deserve a treat! This rigorous logic easily persuades me to do what I already want to do.

Searching a pocket inside the pack I locate my tiny army-surplus can opener. Three days of hammering and hauling have left my fingers battered and clumsy, but with careful work I get the can half open and bend back the lid. The fish is packed in water, so I first drink the briny liquid. It's incredibly delicious, satisfying a need for salt I didn't know I had. Then, using a horizontal piton as a spoon, I enjoy every succulent bite. It's deeply satisfying and feels like a real meal. For dessert I pick out some gumdrops from the gorp bag.

Today's work is finally done. While I was intent on tuna, the daylight faded away, and night has arrived. Now I sit here, dangling under the roof, suspended in the inky darkness.

Neither twinkling star nor hint of moonlight glimmers through the moist blanket of clouds above me. In the blackness below, cars move slowly along the roads, their lights glistening on the wet pavement. The people in those automobiles seem very far away. They're in a different world, a horizontal existence of speed, destinations, and obligations. High on this wall, what do I care whether it's today or yesterday? Alone, serving only the laws of steep rock, I find something as precious as water to a man stranded in the desert: I find freedom.

There's something else, less admirable. Up here I can freely indulge the sin of pride by looking down on my fellow humans. Up here I easily forget we are all hurtling with the same velocity toward the grave and its worms. Climbers are proud of going places and spending nights where millions of Yosemite visitors can never go. Tourists are confined to roads and trails, to lodges and campgrounds. Climbers don't need cabins or houses on wheels. We sleep happily on the ground, and on ledges – when we can find one – and we can go for days on what tourists eat in one meal. Instead of the god of security, we bow to the greater god of freedom, the freedom to take risks and master danger in order to be intensely alive.

When I am down there, in the flatlands, I am an anonymous citizen, subject to the same physical laws and social rules as everyone else. But up here it's different. I own this vertical world. I have paid for it with brute effort and what courage I could muster. Where is the deed to my property? Only in my mind.

Enough. I rest my shoulder and ski-capped head against the granite wall and, in the time-honored tradition of mountaineers around the world, am quickly asleep.

Sometime later I awaken to find that my feet have gone numb from the pressure of my aid slings. I tap my toes against the rock, then flail them in the air like some uncoordinated swimmer until circulation is restored. Then I put my feet back in the slings and wait for sleep to return.

I think of Liz. And of us. We seem made for each other. Being a dreamer, I need a smart, practical woman to guide me through the maze of the "real" world. She responds to a man who has a compelling passion that is even greater than his need for her. With me, it's climbing. She has already rebuffed guys who threatened to stifle her fierce spirit of independence. She won't be owned. She will be married, though. We'll do it soon. It'll be forever....

The next time I wake up I find that my legs as well as my feet have gone to sleep. They don't seem to understand that *I'm* supposed to be doing the sleeping here! I stand up, rubbing my legs and kicking the wall until feeling comes back. This winter we'll work on better gear for hanging bivies.

I resume my sitting position. It's a good thing I'm blessed with the knack for dozing in places that would give most people the heebie-jeebies. Still, I wouldn't mind having a ledge. The Tower is giving me a final test. I can't complain. It's a fair price to pay for a wall like this.

As I wait for sleep I start wondering what Warren and Glen and Al were thinking up here. All those days, hanging in space. They must love it as much as I do....

. . .

Dawn arrives, gray and misty, pushing the darkness away. Clouds hang on the Valley rim. I watch as ragged shreds of vapor drift slowly and silently across the ageless walls.

Standing up in my slings, I have a good stretch. My legs are cramped, my butt is numb, my back is sore, and my neck is stiff – aside from that I feel fine! My head is clear. That's the important thing. My mind will give the orders and my body will follow them.

I munch some gorp. There's not much left. I already picture myself back in Camp 4, at a banquet: all the delicious hot food I can hold, all the wine I could want, a whole night of sleep on flat ground, maybe all day, too.

Quit dreaming! I tell myself. Get to work!

After shoving the bivy gear into the pack, I concentrate on my mess of hardware, crisply clipping everything into place on my carrying sling: knifeblades in front, then horizontals, angles in the middle, then the wide angles and bong-bongs. RURPS and fifi hooks next, carabiners after that, then the runners and tie-offs. All my weapons need to be in the right place for a quick draw.

The roof is about 30 feet above me, a dark triangle jutting out horizontally 20 feet from the wall. I nail up a crack to the roof, fighting past a tough little tree that doesn't want me to pass. Under the ceiling a wide crack goes left for 15 feet. I will have to drive pitons straight up into this crack to get out to the edge of the roof. I unclip a 3-inch bong and, reaching left, stick it up into the crack. Holding it in place with my left hand, I hammer it with my right. All my weight is on my swami belt, and I'm gasping for air. The piton makes bell-like peals as I strike it. With each blow the note goes higher on the musical scale, the sign of a solid pin. But it's scary too – pins driven straight up don't shift first to warn of failure; they just pop out.

I clip in and gingerly transfer my weight to the piton. It holds. I unclip another bong and reach out left. Stretching as far as I can, I wedge it up into the crack where it sticks without my having to hold it in place. Transferring the hammer to my left hand, I aim at the head of the piton but fail to land a square blow. As the hammer glances off, the pin jerks sideways, pops out of the crack, and drops silently into the void. I watch it fall, turning end over end, until it is too small to see. I listen intently but can't hear it hit the ground.

One little mistake and it's gone. What if it were me? Would I fall so silently, or would I scream all the way down?

Cautiously, I continue the traverse, placing the bongs closer together so I can hold on to each one as I hammer it. When I reach the left edge of the roof I look up to see what appears to be a good ledge, 30 feet higher. A piton crack leads up 10 feet and then disappears, leaving 20 feet of free climbing. Free climbing? Just me and the rock? I wasn't expecting this. At least it doesn't look too hard, but what a wild place to step out of aid slings.

I nail up the crack and then, suspended from my top piton, carefully judge the distance to the ledge. Yes ... just about 20 feet. On this section I'll need to keep one hand holding onto the rock for balance, but it takes two hands to loosen the prusik knots, slide them along the rope, and then tighten them again. So I pay out 25 feet of slack and cinch up the knots, extra tight. Now I'll be able to gain the ledge without moving the prusiks, but any fall will be 25 feet, maybe 50.

Hmmm....

I reach down and drive in another piton, just below my top one. Now I'm ready to go for it, but first I double-check my tie-in and prusiks, and make sure the loop of slack won't catch on anything. It's all OK. Then I find some handholds, step out of my aid slings, and start up, moving from hold to hold. I know how to play this game. It's all mental. Relax, don't rush it, and pretend you're only 10 feet off the ground.

In a few minutes I am at the ledge. Whew!

I study the next pitch. It's an overhanging corner – of course. There's a roof in it – of course. I nail up the corner, pass the roof, and continue to where the crack traverses left, under another roof – of course! Will it never end?

The pitch finishes on a good ledge. Above it, 30 feet of easy-looking free climbing leads to what might be the top. I surge up the rock and pull over the edge to find myself looking down the other side of the Tower to Bridalveil Creek far below. This is it! I'm up, floating on a cloud of exhilaration.

How I love these moments of sweet victory on the summit of the Tower! It's been a long journey for the kid who dreamed he could become a climber. Tears of joy bead in my eyes. At last I've silenced the inner voices of self-doubt and self-condemnation. I find myself swimming in a sea of contentment.

Then I realize it's too early to celebrate: I still have work to do. My rope and gear remain on the last pitch. A serpentine voice hisses into my ear, "Just leave it!" but I know I have got to finish the job. Following the routine I've learned so well, I make one last rappel into the void and clean the pitch, removing every piton. Back on top I easily pull up the pack, now containing little food and no water. The climb is finally over. Or is it?

SEEDS OF CONTEMPLATION

In a crossword puzzle I did recently, one of the clues was "Half a mountaineering expedition." It took me a while to get the answer, which was "ascent." Before I reach the Valley I will learn the importance of the other half.

Slowly, one loop at a time, I coil the ropes on which my life has depended. Then I sit on the summit and gaze out over the landscape, nibbling the last bit of jack cheese. The rain has stopped and the layer of clouds has risen, revealing the summits of the great rocks. All the way up the wall, a jingle from a radio ad has been tormenting me:

"You'll wonder where the yeller went, when you brush your teeth with Pepsodent!" A reaction, I suppose, to the constant stress of unremitting concentration. Now I can turn off the white-hot mental intensity I have maintained for four days. At last I can quiet my mind. Worries about falling, forgetting to clip in, a knot coming untied – all those anxieties common to life in the realm of the overhang are behind me. I never did make that one little mistake.

It's still early afternoon; I can relax and soak up the scenery. I look down into the abyss from which I have just emerged. The wall curves in underneath me. I can't see where I started. But I can see Bridalveil Meadow. It's a patch of pure green velvet; I want to roll around in it. Maybe tomorrow I will.

West of the meadow, the Merced River twists and turns, heading toward the flatlands. Across the way, Ribbon Fall bursts from the Valley rim, plunging down in a thick column of surging water. It's a magnificent sight. In my euphoric state, I see nothing ominous about it.

To the right of Ribbon, beyond Lower Cathedral Rock, looms El Capitan. Despite its huge size, it looks like *one stone*, the ultimate monolith. Some of my life's best days have been spent there.

I gaze at my closer neighbors, the three Cathedral Rocks. From the Valley floor, they present a magnificent array of walls and buttresses. But seen from the Tower, they offer only brushy slopes of no interest to climbers. I am, however, very interested in the notch between Lower and Middle Cathedral Rocks – the Gunsight. It's my gateway back to the Valley. To reach it I'll descend the Tower's regular route and then a gully leading to Bridalveil Creek. After hopping across the stream, it will be a simple trudge up to the Gunsight.

Rappelling into the abyss

Before starting down, I take one last look at my favorite landscape. I recall the story of one of the first white men to see Yosemite: Looking down from the rim, he burst into tears, overcome by the beauty of the Incomparable Valley.

I know how he felt. For ten years Yosemite has given me everything. It's been a playground and a battleground, calling forth my best efforts, showing me what lies within. For this I left a steady job with a secure future. Today I know that step into the unknown was the right choice.

CROSSING OVER

With the pack on my back and a rope around each shoulder, I start down, looking for Charles Michael's original route. It's good old-fashioned route finding, zigzagging down slabs and cracks. At the hardest places I use my slings to lower the pack to a ledge before climbing down. After reaching the gully I scramble down and soon I am standing on the bank of Bridalveil Creek – appalled.

The "creek" is roaring by in full flood. I can't believe my eyes. I knew it would be high, but not like this! Wide-eyed, I study the river's headlong descent. It goes over a sharp drop just below me. Then it sprays across polished slabs to another drop, before again sweeping powerfully across more slabs as if shot from a giant fire hose. The torrent plunges a hundred yards farther before springing into the air to become Bridalveil Fall.

I can't see it, but I know the water drops 600 feet before shattering on the rocks below into sheets of spray and clouds of mist. That's

"Bridalveil Fall, Yosemite Valley, Yosemite Sierra", ca. 1927   *Photo: Ansel Adams*

what the tourists come to see. If only I were down there with them.

I stare across at the far bank. It's just 30 feet away. Reach it and all my problems are solved. On summer days I've dallied in this stream, swimming in its quiet, sybaritic pools. Now all the confidence I've gained from climbing the Tower is being swept downstream by the rushing water. I admit it – I'm scared. All I can do is go upstream and hope for something better.

Fighting my way through brush and scrambling across slabs, I work upriver looking for a place to cross. I'm stopped by a cliff. I could climb around it, but then what? Snow covers the creek drainage above, and I picture myself plodding uphill through snow in my tight rock shoes. No, that won't do. I wouldn't get anywhere anyway, unless I went all the way up to the Glacier Point Road, several miles away. But that's the wrong way. I want to go toward the Valley, not away from it.

Stymied, I study the moving water, noting that the stream here is wider and less deep, the water moving a little slower than on the steeper sections below. Instead of skimming slabs, it passes over the rounded stones and boulders of a typical Sierra stream. With the lip of the fall now farther away, I feel braver. Perhaps I can wade here. Upstream, a Jeffrey pine stands on the bank. That's the answer. A rope around the tree will provide a safety line so I can wade across. I don't have much experience with this sort of thing, but it looks simple enough.

Trembling with anticipation, I uncoil the 9 mm rope and pass it around the tree, as if for a rappel. I leave my shoes on for better traction on the loose, slippery rocks in the streambed.

Crossing Bridalveil Creek

Thirty feet below the pine, holding onto the doubled rope with both hands, I step into the stream, facing the far shore, determined to get there. Ice water immediately fills my shoes, but it's a cheap toll to pay for this river crossing. I grit my teeth and move out into the current, letting the rope slide through my hands as I press forward. I can't see the creek bed because of the swirling water. I have to go by touch, advancing one foot, feeling for a secure spot among the stones, then doing the same with the other. I wouldn't dare try this without the rope; coming down from the tree it gives me support and confidence. Already the far bank, the promised land, is coming closer.

Suddenly a stone rolls under my left foot. Teetering, arms swinging wildly in the air, I almost let go of the rope. Staggering like a besotted fool, I barely stay on my feet. That was close!

I stop and steady myself: nerves, body, brains – yes, they're all still here, just a little scrambled. Slow down, I tell myself. Don't rush it. And stop looking at that far shore. Don't even think about it. The only important thing is the next step.

As I move into deeper water the relentless current, now nearly to my knees, seems intent on sweeping me away, as if I were a trespasser entering forbidden territory. My heart pounds as I realize that the rope, now running diagonally from the tree, is becoming my enemy. With each step I take, it offers less support. Waves are now lapping over the rope, tugging on it, pulling me back.

The torrent is overpowering. My feet are so numb it's like walking on stumps. I must not fall. I won't be able to get back up. The current will hold me down until, drowning, I let go of the rope and take that nightmare ride down the slabs and over the brink.

Stalled halfway across the river, I don't know what to do. Panic surges through me. All I can think is: Drop the rope! Run for it! But I don't give in. The merciless current would sweep me away before I could take half a step.

I've never seen death so close. After all those wild things on rock – I never thought it would be water. I'm not giving up, but I just don't have any answers. I can't last much longer. I cry out, "Please, God, save me!"

I attempt one more step. This time I lift my foot all the way out of the water, and am amazed to find myself in balance. Am I dreaming? Is this how prayers are answered? Suddenly I understand: When I raise a foot high, all my weight is on one leg, cutting in half the water's power to pull me down. As long as one leg is in the air I won't get swept away. Yet it's nearly impossible to stand on one foot in this surging water. But I have no choice – I *have* to stand on one foot. I tell myself it's like bouldering without using my hands, where I discover how many limbs I can do without. This is a new situation, but I'm learning fast – I have to.

As I put my left foot down, the powerful flow pushes against both legs, each carrying half the weight of my body. I fight to stay upright until I can raise my right foot. Up it goes, and I stop teetering. As I set it back down, the current grips both legs again and almost snatches them from under me. So it goes, one tortured step at a time, like Buster Keaton on a high wire.

Just a few more steps, then the water gets shallower, the current eases, and at last I stagger onto dry land. I slump down on a boulder, take a deep breath, and look back at the torrent. Bridalveil Creek has washed away any arrogance that might have grown out of my success on the Tower. I am freshly humbled.

Nevertheless, now that I'm out of danger, I forget to thank God for mercy. It is said that there are no atheists in foxholes. I think there are none in the middle of raging rivers, though there might be agnostics along the shore.

I haul in the rope and coil it. Then, shouldering both ropes and the pack, I climb up through manzanita and live oak to the Gunsight. At the notch I look down into the Valley; I'm almost home. El Capitan rises on the other side. I briefly scan the vast canvas of its unclimbed southeast face. *Someday, maybe.* Then I start down the dark, narrow gully. The rock is wet and slippery. Newly aware of the value of just being alive, I avoid climbing down anything risky. Uncoiling my 9 mm rope, I rappel over a big chockstone, retrieve the rope, and then work my way down the steep gully, warning myself repeatedly to stay alert. The gully ends, and now it's just forested talus. I recall my slip on the approach, four days ago; for the last time I tell myself to be careful.

And then it is truly over. The ground becomes gently sloping and then flat as I reach the road and find myself walking along the banks of the Merced, once more in Eden. The Valley is the same as when I started. Nothing has changed, except me – I am more confident. I am aware that I have mastered myself.

At El Cap Meadow I look back at the Gunsight. Nestled in the "V" of its notch, the summit of the Tower rises in the distance. I respectfully nod to it.

It's such a relief, walking along the road, not having to examine the ground for footholds at every step. The landscape changes rapidly as I pace eastward. Soon the walls of the upper Valley come into view but for once I don't analyze them in my usual way; I need something else.

Suddenly a giant of a man comes striding toward me out of the forest. It's Layton Kor, the phenomenon from Colorado, a titan of American climbing.

"Robbins!" he shouts. "Where have you been?"

"On the Leaning Tower."

"I knew it. As soon as I saw all that gear, I knew it. You've been up there all this time? In this weather?"

"Yeah," I reply, trying to act casual.

"Fantastic! That's amazing. Congratulations!"

"Thanks, Layton. Thanks." His praise means a lot to me.

I walk on toward Camp 4 and Liz. I'm looking forward to a feast, a jug of red, and holding her close. Tomorrow we will do a climb for pleasure ... well, maybe not tomorrow. Tomorrow I will have a great time doing absolutely nothing. Then we will take that pleasure cruise, just the two of us, moving lightly over the rock, just for the fun of it. It's the other side of climbing.

By and by, the call of the big walls will return, and I'll respond. For now, I am content. I'm in balance. When that equilibrium gets tipped, as it always does, I will return to the vertical world.

To hard rock, thin air, a rope.

Yosemite Valley　　　　　　　　　　　　　　　　　*Photo: Glen Denny*

Two non-profit agencies are very close to my heart. These are the Yosemite Fund and the Boy Scouts of America. The Boy Scouts, as recounted in these pages, made a positive difference in my life at a time when a difference needed to be made. For young men the Boy Scouts is the leading organization in the United States. And the Yosemite Fund is the preeminent supporter of Yosemite National Park, where I have spent a lot of time and where I have done many climbs. But the Fund is more than an effective steward that implements projects in the Park that would otherwise not be done. It is an organization of very successful individuals who share a passion for Yosemite. I am attracted to this group because it is effective, its members love Yosemite, and they do everything with excellence. I hope you will support these two meritorious, philanthropic organizations.

Cordially,
Royal Robbins

APPENDIX

ACCIDENT ON THE LEANING TOWER

More than 30 years after Harding's close call on the Tower, a similar but more serious accident struck. Brad Young was more than half-way up the wall when he dislodged a flake that hit his partner, Doug Burton. It fell free 20 feet and struck Doug's (luckily) helmeted head. Helmets are rarely worn in Yosemite, especially on an overhanging wall, where the danger of rock fall seems remote. Not so remote as one might think, judging by these near-death experiences. This accident also shows the difficulty of rescue on the Tower.

Brad sent me the following account:

The accident happened on July 4, 1992, on the third pitch above Ahwahnee Ledge. The pitch consists of discontinuous seams with abundant loose flakes. I was 15 feet above Doug, and tried to place a camming unit [a modern, adjustable substitute for a piton] behind a flake. Suddenly the flake fractured and slid off. I yelled "Rock!" and saw the flake hit Doug in his forehead as he looked up.

It all happened instantly and blood was everywhere. Doug was unconscious. I had to climb down to Doug, which took a while. I yelled at him again and again and then he came to consciousness. I took off my headband and stuffed it under his helmet, which was cracked from rim to center, and covered with hair and blood.

Doug was in fairly good spirits, almost insouciant, but I in contrast was stiff with fear. At this point we were about 300 feet down from the top of the Tower, 1,500 feet off the deck, on a massively overhanging wall. I started yelling for help.

I don't think I have ever felt so completely helpless as trying to yell from the Leaning Tower for help, over roaring Bridalveil Fall. We yelled for what seemed like hours.

Eventually, we heard a siren, and for the first time in my life, I was overjoyed to see a ranger car in Yosemite Valley with full flashing lights. I heard a ranger on a bullhorn, who identified himself as John Dill.

I cannot praise Dill's handling of the rescue enough. From the first minutes of his communication by bullhorn, it was obvious why he is called the "Guru" of Yosemite Search and Rescue. The rescue itself was probably straightforward for the Search and Rescue people. They lowered a ranger down from the summit (which they reached by helicopter) and he hung 50 feet out in space. He threw me a ball of twine, and I sent out my haul rope and hauled him in. We got Doug into a litter and he was lowered to the ground where it took three hours to evacuate him to the parking lot. He was helicoptered to Modesto where doctors performed surgery to repair a broken skull, 23 hours after he was hurt. Doug recovered relatively quickly, and is now mostly okay, except for a dent and a scar on his forehead.

DANGEROUS CROSSINGS

That my apprehension while crossing Bridalveil Creek was not merely the product of an inflamed imagination is shown by the following fatalities.

The first incident is reprinted from *Accidents in North American Mountaineering*, 1974, published by the American Alpine Club.

California, Yosemite Valley. *On May 29th Richard Jack (age 28) and Peter Williamson (29) completed an ascent of the Grade V route on the Leaning Tower. On their descent they camped for the night at Bridalveil Creek. In the morning they prepared to cross the creek by having one man cross on foot while belayed. Then they would rig a Tyrolean traverse on which the packs and the second man could cross. Williamson removed his clothes, put on his swami belt and seat harness, tied in, and entered the water. He was rapidly swept away and under. Jack was unable to help. He tied off the belay line, attached a second line to it, and finally pulled Williamson's body to shore. (Source: Peter Thompson.)*

Analysis: *The precise spot where Williamson entered the water is unknown, but for a mile above Bridalveil Fall the creek runs in excess of twenty knots. The water temperature was estimated to have been well below 50 degrees. The climbers could have chosen one of two other, unattractive descent routes: five miles of unpleasant bushwhacking to the Glacier Point Road or rappel down the loose and dangerous Leaning Chimney. They knew the* *difficulties of these two routes. They did not appreciate the great hazards of river crossings.*

The second incident took place on the middle fork of the Salmon River in Idaho. Don Wilson, a friend of mine and climbing companion in the early 1950s, with whom I made the first free ascent of the Open Book at Tahquitz and the second ascent of the North Face of Sentinel Rock in Yosemite, drowned in the 1970s on a trip down the Salmon River. His party's raft became trapped on an island, and Don attempted to swim across to the bank with a rope to effect a rescue. He was swept downstream and held under by the rope until he drowned.

The moral of these three river stories, including my own, is that the rope, which to climbers means "safety," can be a very dangerous tool in moving water.

SCOUTMASTERS

Looking back on my two Scoutmasters, I realize what a critical difference they made in my life and how much I owe them. As I think about it, I see that it's good men, generous with their time and energy, who make Scouting happen. It's not Scouting per se. Scouting is a vehicle through which good men change forever the lives of boys, and are forever remembered for doing so.

Phil Bailey, Scoutmaster of the Rainbow Troop

Late in 1999 I visited Phil Bailey at his home in the Thousand Oaks Hills above the Simi Valley, north of Los Angeles. Nestled against a rocky, brush-covered hillside, the house is daily visited by rabbits, deer, quail, coyotes, raccoons, and many species of birds. As I drove up the driveway, Phil came to his front steps and greeted me with a smile. Though it had been 50 years since we last met, I recognized him instantly – that smile, the alert, bright eyes, the face from which beamed a reservoir of good will. He'd had some trouble with eyes and legs but was, at age 77, still full of energy and passion for life. All these years he had continued to have a love of the Scouting movement.

Phil had built the world's most complete collection of international Scout uniforms. Now the time had come to transfer the collection to a new Boy Scout museum in Las Vegas. Phil was vexed with contrary feelings about the transfer: Pride that the collection was to be seen and appreciated by far more people, and regret bordering on sadness that the uniforms so dear to his heart were passing from his hands. Phil had entered Scouting at age 18, when he became an assistant cubmaster of a Cub pack and then an assistant Scoutmaster of a Scout troop in Los Angeles. He worked with the two units for several years during World War II, while he was being rejected for military service as "too skinny." Eventually, in 1944, he was accepted. Phil jokes that the Army finally letting him enlist meant the war was either going well or going badly.

He served briefly at Fort Bliss, Texas, and then was sent to Officer Candidate School where he was commissioned in the Corps of Military Police. It is, to me, an amazing coincidence that both my Scoutmasters, one in the Army and one in the Air Force, were stationed at Fort Bliss, where, years later, I was to pass most of my Army time. Phil was dispatched to Europe in 1945, just in time for VE (Victory in Europe) Day. Since he was no longer needed to defeat Hitler, he was re-routed, without his knowledge, to a still-hot theater of operations: Asia. To his surprise, the plane landed in North Africa, then proceeded through the Middle East, past India, over the "Hump" of the Himalayas and into Kunming, the back door of China. A few months later the war with Japan suddenly ended, and his company was moved into the great city of Shanghai to protect American interests. There he met a "grand old English gentleman" named Sandy Gordon. Sandy had become a local hero in Shanghai by being a clandestine Scoutmaster of kids whose parents were stranded in Shanghai for the duration of the war. Under the Japanese occupation, running a Scout troop was an offense punishable by death.

When the Japanese moved into Shanghai in 1941 Sandy was put into prison along with all other citizens of countries at war with Japan. He was upgraded from concentration camp to house arrest because of his usefulness to the Japanese in running the infrastructure of Shanghai. Sandy had been an expert in this area prior to the war.

He had a guard whose job was not to leave his side, but Sandy artfully conned the Japanese soldier into letting him go for evening "walks." On these "strolls" he led the Scout troop. On the day after the Japanese surrendered, some 100 boys and young men, wearing their tattered Scout uniforms, tore the front gates off the fence of the #1 compound, right in front of armed Japanese soldiers.

Phil was inspired when he heard of Sandy Gordon and of this incident. It suggested a level of esprit de corps in Scouting beyond anything he had seen, and he was eager to learn how a Scout leader could build such enthusiasm. His commanding officer was aware of Phil's past experience in Scouting and asked him to rekindle the fire under a Troop that had been part of the Shanghai American School prior to the war but had disbanded when the Japanese arrived. Under Phil's leadership, Shanghai Troop 12 was reborn in March 1946.

For guidance he went to Sandy who admonished him that the aim of Scouting was to teach boys self-reliance. He didn't think it good for boys to be coddled or mothered. "If they get splinters in their hands, don't take them out. Let them take out their own splinters. If they get a scratch, let them pad it themselves. What are we raising? A bunch of ninnies? Let them make mistakes if it isn't a threat to their lives. There's no greater way for them to learn than to have to clean up their own bloody mess."

He thought shorts the proper Scouting outfit. "Long pants will be the ruination of American Scouting. Scouts don't feel special in long pants. Shorts make them feel different. Besides, you can look good in shorts." These and other reflections of Sandy Gordon's would strongly influence Phil when he would return to the United States. In the meantime he rebuilt the troop in Shanghai and, because of its success, was sent to do the same in Peking, Nanking, and eventually Tokyo.

When he was decommissioned, he returned to Los Angeles and enrolled in the Police Academy. After graduating, he was directing traffic in downtown Los Angeles (a rite of passage for graduates) when his sergeant picked him up and asked him if he had ever been in Scouting. When Phil said he had, the sergeant said, "Good, you're our new Scoutmaster."

The year was 1947. They went to a troop meeting at Los Angeles City College, and when they arrived, the seven members of Troop 127 were having a shoe fight. After things quieted down, Phil told the kids, "We're going to have a great Scout troop!" The boys seemed bored to death, and Phil later learned he was the sixth Scoutmaster in a row who had started off his first meeting with that statement. Bailey, however, was as good as his word. Through his leadership, Troop 127 became a "great Scout troop."

I joined Troop 127 a year later. Mr. Bailey was to make an important contribution to my life for which I would be forever grateful.

Al Wilkes, Scoutmaster of Troop 121

At the time he was my Scoutmaster, Al Wilkes worked as an architect. When I visited him in 1999 he was still active in his profession at age 78.

Al grew up in Los Angeles with a dad he described as "falling apart," and a mother who was "very strong." Thinking to ensure good role models for little Al, she got him involved in Scouting. He was barely twelve when he was admitted to Troop 121, after 3 months training in becoming a "Good Scout." Right away, Al felt there was something special about the Scouts. He was impressed with the ideals, with the Scout Laws, with the demands that he measure up.

Al and his fellow Scouts in Troop 121 wore wool uniforms and silk neckerchiefs. Many worked hard to earn money to buy their Scouting outfits. Wilkes attended Los Angeles City College in 1939 and 1940 and worked at Lockheed Aviation before moving on to UCLA in 1941, where he studied architecture and raced on the UCLA Ski Team. He made Eagle Scout and served as assistant Scoutmaster before entering the Army Air Force in World War II in 1942.

In the Army Air Force, Al was a navigator on bombers. Stationed at Bliss Field, El Paso, Texas, he had a close call. The B-29 to which he was assigned crashed on take-off, killing all the crewmen. Luckily, on that day he wasn't flying.

After the war, he returned to Scouting and became Scoutmaster of his old Troop 121. Like Phil Bailey, Al was strongly influenced by Clem Glass, the Scoutmaster of the Air.

Al's goal was to lead a troop that would get outdoors and have adventures. Although he was less keen on drill and "spit and polish" than some Scout leaders, he nevertheless felt the Scout rituals were important and should be honored with spirit and good form.

When I visited him, he didn't seem to have changed much. He appeared fit as ever. His lovely wife, Winnie, who used to be involved in our Scout activities, also was healthy and spry. Winnie was a rare individual in my Scouting days—a Scoutmaster's wife who went on the outings. None of us ever questioned her presence, but there were those on the Los Angeles Scout Council who did. Al also came under question for taking us climbing, an activity then viewed as overly dangerous. Like Phil Bailey, Al courted trouble from his superiors by doing things on the cutting edge. Risks were taken, but that's what made it an adventure. I wouldn't have lasted long in either troop if they had treated us as "ninnies."

For years Winnie and Al competed in the refined and highly disciplined world of ballroom dancing. They have had a great life together and are now living atop a hill in the Santa Monica Mountains above West Los Angeles, near their son, Evan, a builder who often works with Al.

AID SLINGS – See **ETRIERS**.

ANORAK – A waterproof jacket with a hood, worn over a sweater or down jacket, used to protect a climber in stormy weather.

BELAY – Belaying is the method by which, from a secure stance, one climber protects another with the rope. If the person climbing falls, it is the belayer's job to stop the fall by holding onto the rope. There are various positions and techniques for belaying, but the main idea in all of them is to produce enough friction so that the belayer can stop the fall and hold the fallen climber. There are also various methods for a solo climber to protect himself or herself by means of self-belays.

BIVOUAC – In climbing, this term (also called "bivy") refers to a night spent on the mountain without camping gear. The climber tries to keep dry and warm with an anorak, a sweater, and perhaps a down jacket. Sometimes a "bivouac sac" (a waterproof envelope designed to hold one or two climbers) is used.

BOLT – Bolts are placed by drilling a hole in the rock, from 1/4 to 3/8 inch wide and 1 to 2 inches deep. Historically, this was tedious work using a hand drill, but battery-powered alternatives are now available. With expansion bolts, one places in the drilled hole a sleeve of soft metal with a hanger attached, and then drives in a nail that expands the sleeve against the sides of the hole. Compression bolts are preferred in hard rock. These bolts have the advantage of being a single piece of metal with flanges that bulge out from the shaft to a size bigger than the drilled hole. When the bolt is driven into the hole, the flanges are compressed, giving the bolt great holding power. In soft rock, however, the flanges do not compress; instead, they chip the rock away, leaving a loose bolt. For soft rock, such as sandstone, expansion bolts are preferred. Bolts, with their hangers, are normally left in place.

CARABINER – A snap link, somewhat like a big safety pin, used to attach a rope to a piton or other device that has been fixed in rock or ice. Carabiners are also useful for other purposes, such as carrying pitons on slings around one's shoulder. They were originally steel but for many years now have been made of lighter-weight aluminum alloy. Some carabiners have a locking gate for greater safety.

DIRECT AID CLIMBING – Also called aid climbing, this term refers to the technique of climbing by using artificial aids such as pitons, bolts, or other gadgets to support one's body weight when the rock lacks hand and foot holds. If the cracks are good, and the angle not beyond the vertical, aid climbing is usually easy. But when the cracks are shallow and bottoming, or otherwise resistant to pitons, or when the rock is sharply overhanging, aid climbing can be fiendishly difficult.

ETRIERS – Short "ladders," made of loops of nylon webbing, used in direct aid climbing. The climber clips them into pitons or bolts in the wall and steps up from one loop to the next. Etriers originated in Europe using cords thinner than climbing rope and stirrups formed by metal rungs.

FIFI HOOK – This is a metal hook that can be attached to the top of an etrier. It is sometimes used instead of a carabiner. The hook has a small hole in the top to which a thin cord is tied, allowing the climber to retrieve the etrier from above, without descending. Fifi hooks can also be used for direct aid on knobs and tiny ledge-holds, taking the place of a piton or bolt.

FREE CLIMBING – This term refers to climbing rock using only the natural holds. One can use as many points of protection (e.g., pitons, runners, bolts, etc.) as one wishes. As long as they are not used for support, it is still considered free climbing. This is in distinction to aid climbing, where pitons or other devices are used for progress.

GRIPPED – This term refers to a climber who is tense with fear and uncertainty. The ideal is to be relaxed and confident. "Gripped" is the opposite of the ideal.

LIEBACK – A method of climbing a vertical crack whereby the climber presses his feet against one wall and pulls on the edge of the crack with his fingers, thus working his way upward by using constant opposite pressure.

MANTLE – A strenuous gymnastic maneuver in which the climber pulls up on a ledge, switches his arms from pulling up to pushing down, raises a foot to the ledge, and then stands up on it.

NAILING – Another word for "pitoning." When one "nails" a crack, one ascends it by placing pitons and using them for aid.

NUT – An artificial chockstone, usually metal, designed to slot into a crack that narrows downward. The British came up with this device as an alternative to pitons. Like pitons, they come in many sizes. When placed properly, the nut can provide as good protection as a piton, but without damaging the rock. A more modern development is the camming device. This nut has movable parts that press outward against the sides of a crack. When weight is applied, the parts (teeth) press outward even more strongly. Nuts were first used in Yosemite in the late 1960s.

PITCH – A pitch, or lead, is the distance between belay stances on a climb. A pitch can be quite short, but usually it is closer to a rope length. In the 1960s, this was from 100 to 150 feet.

PITON – Pitons are metal spikes, usually made of hard steel, driven into cracks in rock for security or progress. They come in different sizes and shapes, from knife-blades (well named because they are so thin) to bong-bongs (so named because they make bell-like sounds when struck with a hammer) that fit cracks up to 5 or 6 inches wide. Pitons have now been largely replaced by nuts and camming devices.

PRUSIK – A knot developed by the Austrian Karl Prusik. With this knot, one can attach slings to a climbing rope and ascend the rope by sliding the knot upward with the fingers, and then applying weight to the sling, which causes the knot to tighten and hold fast.

PRUSIKING – Climbing a rope by using Prusik knots and slings. This was the method of climbing ropes before mechanical ascenders, such as Jumars, were invented.

RAPPEL – This is a French term meaning "to recall." To rappel, one slides down a rope using a device that creates enough friction to control the speed of descent. Most rappelling is done using a doubled rope, allowing one to pull on one end to retrieve (recall) the rope.

ROPE – A rope has long been naturally associated with mountain climbing. Besides its practical uses, the rope symbolizes the spiritual bond between climbers. Unless it breaks, the climbers live or die together. Until World War II, climbing ropes were made of natural fibers such as Manila hemp. These were usually fine for protecting those who came up from below, but could not be relied upon to hold a leader fall, because such a fall could generate enough force to break the rope. Thus, for over 100 years the climbing mantra was "The leader must not fall!"

Nylon ropes were developed in World War II, and after the conflict they were used for climbing. Such ropes had the virtue of being nearly unbreakable because of the inherent elasticity of nylon. All the belayer had to do was hold onto the rope, and its natural stretchiness would absorb the force of the fall. Suddenly, leader falls became a reasonable risk.

The early nylon climbing ropes, like their natural fiber forebears, were of twisted construction, whereby three or so main strands were twisted around each other to form the rope. By the early 1960s, however, Europeans had developed climbing ropes of kernmantel construction that featured a core (kern) of many thin parallel strands, covered with a woven outer case (mantel) that protected the inner core. Such ropes became standard. The original nylon climbing ropes were 120 feet in length by 7/16 inches in diameter. As climbers began climbing smoother walls, where the ledges were farther apart, the standard length went to 150 feet, then to 165 feet (the equivalent of the European 50 meters). Modern kernmantel ropes are even longer and thinner, and they are stronger than ever.

RUNNER – A nylon sling used to used to lengthen the distance between a piton and the climbing rope to reduce drag on the rope. Runners can also be placed around trees, rock knobs, or spikes to protect the leader.

RURP – An acronym standing for Realized Ultimate Reality Piton. A RURP is a tiny, hatchet-shaped piton designed to be hammered into otherwise unusable incipient cracks. They were invented in 1960 by Yvon Chouinard. RURPs made it possible to go places with pitons that formerly would have required bolts.

SWAMI BELT – This fanciful term refers to nylon webbing wrapped many times around one's waist and knotted. The climbing rope is then tied directly to the swami belt rather than around one's waist. The greater width of the swami reduces the shock of a fall on the waist, provides more support when hanging from the rope, and frees more of the rope for climbing.

TIE-OFF – Slings can be used to lessen leverage on pitons that can't be driven in as far as the eye. By tying a sling around the piton close to the rock and clipping a carabiner to the sling instead of to the eye of the piton, one can greatly reduce leverage and, in effect, increase the holding power of the piton.

WEBBING – Strong lengths of 1-inch wide nylon tape used for many climbing purposes, especially slings, etriers, and swami belts. Half-inch webbing was used for tie-offs.

BIBLIOGRAPHY

Books

Best, Dick, and Beth Best, eds. *Intercollegiate Outing Club Association Song-Fest.* New York: R.L Best, 1932.

Bunnell, M.D., and Lafayette Houghton. *Discovery of the Yosemite and the Indian War of 1851.* New York: Fleming H. Revell Company, 1892.

Chesterton, G.K. *The Man Who Was Thursday.* London: J.W. Arrowsmith, 1908.

Dostoevsky, Fyodor. *The Brothers Karamazov.* Translated by Constance Gannett. New York: Macmillan, 1928.

Gray, Thomas. *Elegy Written in a Country Churchyard.* Boston: Estes and Lauriat, 1883.

Henderson, Kenneth. *The American Alpine Club's Handbook of American Mountaineering.* Boston: Houghton Mifflin Company, 1942.

Ullman, James Ramsey. *High Conquest: The Story of Mountaineering.* London: Gollanz, 1942.

Whymper, Edward. *Scrambles Amongst the Alps in the Years 1860-69.* London: John Murray, 1871.

Articles

"Bus Trouble Again Hits Scout Troop." *Los Angeles Times,* July 9, 1950: p. 19

"L.A. Boys Late." *Los Angeles Times,* July 6, 1950: p. 20.

Macdonald, Allan. "Realm of the Overhang." *Sierra Club Bulletin,* December 1962: pp. 5-22.

Fail Falling

We hope you enjoyed *To Be Brave*, the first volume of *Royal Robbins: My Life*. Each book in the *My Life* series highlights the life adventures of Royal Robbins – legendary climber, kayaker, and world-class outdoorsman.

Featured in *Volume II: Fail Falling* are Royal's climbs of Open Book at Tahquitz Rock, and both his second ascent of Sentinel Rock and his first ascent of Half Dome in Yosemite Valley. Royal describes the meaning behind the title of Volume II:

A group of us were trying a 20-foot top-rope problem. We each failed again and again. Though I had tried it repeatedly and wanted it badly, I was ready to give up. After falling off for the fifth time and being lowered to the ground, I sat on a boulder at the bottom of the steep face with my head in my hands asking myself, "How? How can I do it?" As I sat there, with my eyes closed, a picture popped into my mind: I saw my fingers, and they were horizontal. Then they suddenly lifted up. I saw them lifting, and I said to myself "Ah, I see. You're climbing as high as you can, and then you're letting go. What if, next time, you climb as if you are going to make it, without any thought of failure?" What would happen if I changed my attitude and simply believed I could do it? There would be no giving up. If I was going to fail, I would fail falling.

If you'd like to be the first to learn about the next release in the *My Life* series, please visit **www.RoyalRobbinsTheBook.com**.

PINK MOMENT PRESS

P.O. Box 1050, Ojai, California 93024
www.pinkmomentpress.com

Royal Robbins' accomplishments as rock climber and adventurer are legendary. An early advocate of boltless, pitonless clean climbing, he did much to transform the climbing culture to minimize the human impact on the vertical wilderness and protect its natural features.

As a rock-climbing pioneer, he broke through existing standards to create wholly new skill and difficulty levels. In the 1950s, 60s and into the 70s, Robbins established one daring new climb after another, among them many revered classics on Yosemite's Half Dome and El Capitan.

Royal and his wife, Liz, founded the *Royal Robbins Company* in 1968 and sold it 31 years later. A prolific author, he has written two seminal books, *Basic Rockcraft* and *Advanced Rockcraft*, which showcased his skill and climbing ethic and inspired a whole new generation of climbers. Combined, the two books have sold over 400,000 copies. He is also the subject of a biography, *Spirit of the Age*, written by Pat Ament.

Richly entertaining and personal, *To Be Brave*, the first volume of Robbins' life story, holds the reader spellbound with tales of adventure. But for Robbins, the real adventure is the inner one. By focusing upon the minds, emotions, and spirits of those involved, he relates climbing escapades in terms everyone can understand.

Royal and Liz now live in Modesto, California. Their son, Damon, also lives in Modesto. Their daughter, Tamara, has a home in Moab, Utah.